EDITED BY ROBERT WOODS

Printing and Production for Promotional Materials

A James Peters Book
James Peters Associates, Inc.

VAN NOSTRAND REINHOLD COMPANY
New York

Copyright © 1987 by Van Nostrand Reinhold Company Inc.

Library of Congress Catalog Card Number 86-11116

ISBN 0-442-23108-3

Printed in the United States of America
Designed by A. Bostroem Kurz

Van Nostrand Reinhold Company Inc.
135 West 50th Street
New York, New York 10020

Van Nostrand Reinhold Company Limited
Molly Millars Lane
Wokingham, Berkshire RG11 2PY, England

Van Nostrand Reinhold
480 La Trobe Street
Melbourne, Victoria 3000, Australia

Macmillan of Canada
Division of Canada Publishing Corporation
164 Commander Boulevard
Agincourt, Ontario M1S 3C7, Canada

16 15 14 13 12 11 10 9 8 7 6 5 4 3 2 1

Library of Congress Cataloging-in-Publication Data

Woods, Robert, 1953–
   Printing and production for promotional materials.

   Includes index.
   1. Advertising layout and typography. 2. Advertising fliers—Printing. 3. Commercial art—Printing.
4. Graphic arts. 5. Printing, Practical. I. Holtje, Bert. II. Title.
Z257.W66 1986   686.2'24   86-11116
ISBN 0-442-23108-3

Contents

Planning 1
Promotional Projects

The purpose of this book is to expand the reader's knowledge of the mechanisms of printing and production as they relate to the practical needs of promotion. Along with careful planning, it is possible to use printing methods to produce a variety of materials. This chapter will guide you through the planning stages, identify different types of promotional materials, and refer you to subsequent chapters on printing and production techniques.

The Need for Promotion

Broadly defined, promotion is the act of furthering growth or development—in this case, of a company's or organization's products, services, or ideas. Frequently, promotion is accomplished through some form of advertising. Print advertising, in various formats and levels of sophistication, has proven effective in getting promotional messages to prospective buyers.

As diverse as the methods of applying ink to paper are, so too are printed promotional materials diverse. They range from a simple one-page, black-and-white flier heralding a new widget to a glossy-covered, four-color booklet celebrating a company's 100th anniversary.

Knowing how and when to use which type of material is the key to successful promotion. The best way to accomplish this is to devise a plan to help you meet desired goals. Besides knowing how to print promotional materials, there are important decisions—having to do with scheduling, delegating duties, establishing a realistic budget, setting goals and priorities—that will greatly influence the outcome

1

of any promotion. Engineering and sticking to your plan are the first small steps to a winning promotional leap.

Establishing Goals

Once the decision has been made to print promotional material, a plan of execution should be established. Depending on the size and structure of the company or organization, the whole project might be turned over to an advertising agency. But there are many promotional projects that can be handled in-house, without having to incur the costs of hiring an outside agency.

The first step for in-house production is to establish some clear-cut goals and priorities for the promotion. The aim of a printed piece may be to enhance sales of particular products or to maintain the reputation of a company. The specific goals of a single promotion may tie into a larger marketing campaign, so both short-term and long-term goals may have to be considered. In any case, predetermining priorities and goals can influence the choice made from among the various kinds of promotions available. The following list identifies some of the considerations that may influence decision making:

Time: There may only be a certain amount of time in which to develop a project, and some printing and production methods take longer than others.

Quality: Depending on a number of factors, the desired quality of the material must be considered, taking into account such criteria as budget, audience, and format.

Use of color: It is more expensive to print in color, and the preparation is more time-consuming. This can also influence the selection of paper, as well as the binding and finishing techniques. Refer to subsequent chapters on these subjects for further information.

Quantity: Generally speaking, the more copies that are printed, the lower the cost per copy. Likewise, certain printing methods are better suited to large print-runs.

Audience: Whom are you trying to reach, and what kind of influence do you want to establish? Naturally, certain types of materials are designed to attract specialized groups of potential buyers.

It is also paramount that someone be put in charge of the project. Arriving at certain decisions may involve input from any number of groups or individuals, but one person should coordinate the planning and execution. This way, if questions or problems arise, either with outside suppliers such as the typesetter or printer or with someone within the company, one person will always know what is going on.

Planning a Budget

Generally, the desired outcome of the promotion should be worth as much or more than the expense of producing it. As usual, you have to spend money to make money, but how you spend can make the difference between success or failure in the end. Before any money is allocated, it may be necessary to prove that the perceived results will be worth the investment.

Therefore, at the same time that goals are being established, the costs of achieving these goals must be taken into account. For example, if a retailer is planning to promote a one-day sale with a hand-out flier, several printing methods could be used to obtain the same results. But the cost of one compared with the other could be enough to make the decision obvious. Certainly, it will be expensive to create original artwork and text and print them in four colors. On the other hand, a one-page flier can easily and quickly be prepared from existing copy and reproduced on a high-speed copier at a fraction of the cost.

When preparing a budget for a printing project, decide what the production alternatives are and gather cost estimates for each. Consider the following:

Format: Naturally, a pamphlet is more expensive to produce than a flier, for instance, so it is essential to choose what type of format will best get the message across. Various formats will be discussed later in this chapter.

Printing process: Depending on the type of printed material you have in mind, one or more printing methods may be appropriate. Chapter 2 provides information on how to select the right process, and subsequent chapters explain the individual processes, such as letterpress and lithography. The printing method can also determine whether you use one, two, or four colors, as well as the quantity of the print run.

Artwork: You may have to contract an outside artist or photographer and prepare the finished piece for printing. Chapter 8 discusses this procedure.

Typesetting: A typesetting house can provide you with a fairly accurate estimate based on the quantity and complexity of the material to be typeset. Typography is the subject of chapter 9.

Design, layout, and paste-ups: An outside supplier may charge by the hour or by the job to design a project; he or she may or may not also execute the paste-ups. These steps are explained in chapter 10.

Paper: Certain types of paper are used for specific methods of printing (most four-color work, for example, is printed on a glossy sheet) and to achieve different effects. Paper is the subject of chapter 11.

Writing, editing, and proofreading: Even if the copy is produced in-house, you may want to hire the services of an outside editor and/or proofreader prior to typesetting. Charges for these services vary, so estimates are mandatory. Editing and proofreading are discussed in chapter 13.

Binding and finishing: The nature of the project may demand the added expense of custom binding, folding, die-cutting, or finishing work, which may or may not be performed by the printer. Some inexpensive processes can create expensive-looking effects. This topic is discussed in chapter 14.

Distribution: If you are preparing a direct-mail project (the subject of chapter 15) or a printed piece that requires mailing, consider postal charges and the various class rates—for example, first-class versus book rate. Otherwise, charges may be incurred for different kinds of distribution, such as shipping, messenger services, or leafleting by hand.

Placement of advertising: You may want to consider buying advertising space in newspapers, magazines, and other publications that accept paid ads. Rates vary depending on the publication. The subject is discussed later in this chapter.

Miscellaneous costs: Expenses incurred by outside suppliers and for postage, supplies, and other items should be given consideration.

Determining Schedules

After the goals are set and the budget is estimated, a production schedule can be prepared. If a date when the printed material is needed can be fixed, you can use it as a reference point from which to work *backward* in preparing the schedule. Likewise, printers generally set firm dates for when material is due at the plant, when the job will go to press, and when the finished product will be ready for delivery. Deadlines should be given to all outside suppliers.

Many promotional projects require coordination with an overall marketing strategy that may dictate when certain materials are needed. If the project is printed too early, for example, expenses may be incurred for having it stored. Or if the company's business is seasonal, materials may have to be ready in time for that season. The same applies to new-product introductions and promotional materials; the preparation of materials has to coincide with the release of the products.

By coordinating your production schedule with sales projections and production of the products themselves, you can more easily assign realistic deadlines for outside suppliers.

Scheduling production, setting a budget, and deciding on project goals are typically tasks of the overall manager of the project. More details on managing printing projects can be found in chapter 12.

Formats for Printed Promotions

As stated earlier in the chapter, selecting the format of the printed promotion will greatly aid in planning the production. Alternatively, the format may be determined by the time-frame for producing the material. Either way, the format is a focal point in planning. A variety of different formats can be used in printed promotions.

Print Advertising

A common form of advertising, print ads can be placed in newspapers and magazines, often in conjunction with other elements of a marketing campaign, including television ads or outdoor advertising. Direct mail can also be considered print advertising and may include a variety of related printed materials, some of which are discussed here. Direct-mail procedures are the subject of chapter 15.

Certain aspects of placing ads in newspapers and magazines should figure into your planning process, in addition to the production of the ad. For instance, it may be necessary to do some research on which publications represent the best market for your advertising. From an advertiser's point of view, different publications reach very different audiences. Just take a look at any newsstand to get some idea of the high degree of specialization, from daily mass-circulation newspapers to monthly magazines for weight lifters. Naturally, these publications charge different advertising rates, based on a number of demographic criteria. This is the type of information readily handled by advertising agencies, but you can do the research yourself. For example, you can generally telephone any newspaper's advertising department and ask for various rates, either on a one-time or regular contractual basis.

Publications also have certain size requirements for different ads, as well as different requirements for preparation of materials, depending on the printing method. A widely used resource for all such information is Standard Rate and Data Service, which regularly publishes reference volumes providing most of the information you will need. The volumes have distinct titles that reflect the general categories of publications, such as newspapers, consumer magazines, business magazines, and farm magazines. They are usually available at local libraries.

When placing print ads, keep in mind that publications often have seasonal or other special options that may benefit your plans. Newspapers may dedicate certain ad sections to different days of the week—groceries and food on Wednesdays, for example, or housewares on Thursdays. Likewise, some magazines will publish special reports or sections that lend themselves to specific kinds of advertising, such as a special section on computer products. You may also want to inquire about special placement of ads, such as on the back cover or next to the table of contents (for which a higher rate is usually applied).

One-page Promotions
There are a number of uses for one-page promotions, which can be manipulated into a variety of formats. They can be used as parts of larger presentations, accompanied by other promotional material; they can be printed in black-and-white or color by different methods, and on different grades of paper; and they can be folded or otherwise finished to create a range of effects.

Some of the simplest and cheapest one-page promotions can be effectively reproduced on high-speed copying machines, located in-house or at quick-print copy centers; some machines print in more than one color. More complex jobs require the services of a commercial printer. Refer to subsequent chapters on printing processes to help you decide which is best suited to your needs.

Brochures, Booklets, and Pamphlets
If you have more to say than can fit on a single sheet of paper, you can choose from various multipage formats, as well as paper grades (including cover stock in this case) and finishing techniques. Different printers may interchange definitions in this category, so always ask for a printed sample before making any decisions.

Catalogs
Selling products through catalogs is becoming increasingly popular, largely because this greatly lowers the cost of making a sale (the costs of maintaining a personal sales force are discussed in chapter 15). Catalogs vary in size, number of pages, colors, and binding, from the slick Neiman-Marcus treatment for the up-scale audience to the one-color variety printed on newsprint.

Reprints
With minimum expense, you can have published ads or articles reprinted for promotional purposes, sometimes with the option of adding information, such as names of dealers and a toll-free telephone number. If the ad or article has appeared in another publication, it may be possible to obtain a copy of the film or the original mechanical paste-ups. You can also reprint by offset from a tearsheet, although you may have to rescreen the job to avoid a moiré pattern.

Point-of-Purchase Promotions
To attract potential buyers while they wait at the check-out counter, or while they are passing a product on a shelf or have one otherwise within viewing distance, "p-o-p" materials may be considered. These can range in size, material, and design, limited only by budget, a printer's capabilities, and the designer's imagination. But when considering printing on materials such as plastic, metal, or wood, be aware that specialized printing methods may have to be employed. Refer to subsequent chapters on printing techniques and preparation of materials.

Outdoor and Transit Advertising
Like p-o-p materials, outdoor and transit advertising carry an immediate sales message in a dynamic format, often enhanced by special effects such as lighting or fluorescent paints. These too can be produced in a range of sizes and materials. Only certain types of specialized printers handle such jobs. Some localities have restrictions on outdoor advertising, so be sure to inquire before making any plans. Also, rates charged for renting such ad space vary, as do the charges for erecting billboards and other outdoor signs.

Novelty Promotions
This mixed-bag category includes everything from plastic shopping sacks handed out at trade shows to pressure-sensitive labels to silk-screened T-shirts. All help promote your company or products and have the added appeal of being eye-catching. They can be printed on all types of materials, so methods such as screen printing and flexography are often used (see the following chapters for more information on these). Once you find a printer to handle the job, you are limited, again, only by budget and your imagination.

Advertising Organizations

Considering the time and money spent on sales promotions, you may want to consult with a professional organization before making definite plans. A variety of such groups exist, some of which specialize in certain types of promotions, such as p-o-p or outdoor billboards.

Before listing professional, nonprofit groups, a word should be said about advertising agencies. Depending on the scope of your promotion and your budget, an agency may provide solutions that developing the project in-house may not. Agencies specialize in certain types of accounts, such as consumer or industrial, and generally provide much preliminary research, from selecting the proper medium for your ad to writing copy and designing materials.

Nevertheless, many promotions can be executed without the help of an agency, although doing so will require a certain amount of legwork. The following professional organizations can provide useful information, and many maintain invaluable and extensive libraries of promotional materials prepared by member companies and individuals.

Audit Bureau of Circulations, 900 N. Meacham Rd., Schaumburg, IL 60195. An organization that collects and publishes information on magazine circulations.

Advertising Council, 825 Third Ave., New York, NY 10022. A nonprofit group that helps plan and create public-service advertising.

Advertising Research Foundation, 3 E. 54 St., New York, NY 10022. An organization that studies the effectiveness of advertising.

American Association of Advertising Agencies, 666 Third Ave., 13th Floor, New York, NY 10017. Better known as the "4As," this group's members are ad agencies.

American Business Press, 205 E. 42 St., New York, NY 10017. An organization of industrial, trade, and professional publishing companies.

American Newspaper Publishers' Association, The Newspaper Center, 11600 Sunrise Valley Dr., Reston, VA 22091. A trade association of daily and Sunday newspaper publishers.

Association of National Advertisers, 155 E. 44 St., New York, NY 10017. A trade association of leading national advertisers.

Business Publications Audit of Circulation (BPA), 360 Park Ave. South, New York, NY 10010. An organization that audits the circulations of business, trade, and professional magazines.

Newspaper Advertising Bureau, 485 Lexington Ave., New York, NY 10017. An organization that does research and promotion of newspaper advertising.

Direct Mail/Marketing Association (DMMA), 6 E. 43 St., New York, NY 10017. A national group of advertisers that use direct-mail promotions (see also chapter 15).

Point-of-Purchase Advertising Institute (POPAI), 60 E. 42 St., New York, NY 10165. An association of advertisers, agencies, and manufacturers of p-o-p materials.

Standard Rate and Data Service, 3004 Glenview Rd., Wilmette, IL 60091. A company that publishes volumes listing rate structures and other information about magazines and newspapers.

Traffic Audit Bureau, 708 Third Ave., New York, NY 10017. An organization that evaluates audiences for outdoor advertising.

Selecting the Right 2
Printing Process

What is the right printing process for any job? What printing processes have you used in the past several years? Do you feel that you could have done a more effective job if you had known more about the available printing processes?

Chances are that you have used lithography (offset) about 95 percent of the time. Nevertheless, you should have an idea of the capabilities and limitations of the various other printing processes in order to make the most educated decision. Although subsequent chapters will discuss these processes in detail, here we will briefly describe the major printing processes and how to go about choosing the right one. The aim is to provide you with a better understanding of printing and thus broaden your print-purchasing powers.

There are three major printing processes: letterpress, lithography, and gravure. Lesser-used processes include flexography, screen printing, and thermography. In the believe-it-or-not category, I would add the photocopying process.

Letterpress

Letterpress prints from a relief surface, as illustrated in figure 2-1. The raised surface accepts ink and transfers the image to paper, using either a sheet-fed or web press. Generally speaking, the larger the surface, the more ink accepted and the darker the transferred image. Translating that to something easier to understand, think of light and bold type. Bold type accepts more ink than light type and therefore appears darker.

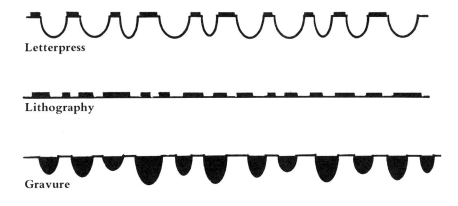

Letterpress

Lithography

Gravure

Figure 2-1. Diagram of the three major printing processes—letterpress, lithography, and gravure—showing the image area in all three.

One of the first steps in letterpress—as in any printing process, really—is to set type. Until the advent of computerized typesetting, most type for the past century was set in hot metal on a Linotype machine. This is accomplished by an operator who presses keys on a typewriterlike keyboard as copy is read. The machine uses circulating matrices and produces each line of type in the form of a solid metal slug. From this process comes the term *hot type,* which is obviously different from photographic or computerized *cold type.* Such computerized methods have largely replaced hot type today. Indeed, no new Linotype equipment is being manufactured anymore.

When an illustration or photograph is to be reproduced by letterpress, a printing plate, known as a *photoengraving,* must be made. When printing a magazine page, for example, the photoengravings and metal slugs are assembled in proper position, locked up, and placed on the bed of the press. When the press is in operation, an ink roller passes over the relief, or printing portions of the form, which in turn transfer its image onto paper. Any slight excess of ink will spill over to the depression or trough formed between the printing surfaces.

This type of letterpress printing is declining in overall importance in the industry. And since hot-metal typesetting is also on the decline, computerized composition has to be converted to photoengraving if used in letterpress printing.

Both type and photoengravings have a limited reproduction life-span due to physical wear. This problem is resolved by molding both the photoengravings and type in an electrotyping process. This not only creates longer-wearing printing plates but also permits the electrotypes to be curved to fit the press cylinders.

The next phase of letterpress is the web process. In web (or roll-fed) printing, a roll of paper is threaded through the printing sections of the press; the feed is continuous until the roll is exhausted. When this is about to happen, a new roll is readied to replace the old one. At the strategic moment, when the roll has wound down almost to its bare core, the two rolls are spliced together with glue. The glued splice releases the spent roll, and the new web of paper continues the printing operation without interruption.

At the delivery end of the press, the web has to be cut, either in sheets or folded segments known as signatures. A very high speed method of printing, a web press runs from 20,000 to 40,000 impressions per hour. A similar web process is also used in lithography and gravure printing.

Lithography

Formally called *offset lithography,* this process is generally referred to as either lithography or, simply, offset. The printing surface is a flat plate, typically made of aluminum, and the printing image is on the surface.

As with letterpress, the more ink accepted by the image area, the darker the reproduction will be. Unlike letterpress, which is a direct-impression type of printing, the lithographic image is first transferred to a blanket cylinder, which *offsets* its image onto paper. Lithography is considered the most versatile method of printing reproduction, both for short and long press-runs.

In this process, everything must be photographed, since the printing plate is a one-piece unit. If there are corrections, the plate must be remade completely. In some cases, where a deletion must be made, small areas can be rubbed off the plate.

The printing process involves a dampening roller running over the plate, at which time the nonimage area accepts moisture. This is followed by an ink roller over the same plate, wherein the image area accepts the ink while the moistened, nonimage areas repel the greasy ink.

As with letterpress, lithography uses both sheet-fed and web presses. The sheet-fed method is used for comparatively short press-runs, up to about 50,000 impressions. With web offset, the cutoff of the roll of paper is similar to that in the letterpress method described earlier.

A brief word about paper used in lithography: because of the moisture factor, the paper must be water-resistant or contain sizing to repel moisture, especially with a sheet-fed press. (The selection of paper is the subject of chapter 11.)

Gravure

Gravure is probably the least understood printing process and is more specialized than either letterpress or lithography. As illustrated in figure 2-1, the printing area is below the plate surface. Furthermore, all materials printed by gravure—type, photographs, or art—must first be screened, or broken up into a series of dot patterns. (Not to be confused with screen printing, the subject of chapter 6, gravure is discussed at length in chapter 5.)

In gravure printing, the ink is very fluid and flows onto the paper readily. The printing surface is incised or engraved into the plate, so the deeper the well, the more ink it will hold and the more ink will flow onto the paper. When printing an illustration, for example, the amount of ink flowing onto the paper enables the ink to overlap, thus giving the appearance of a solid printed area. From this you can gather that the wells must be of various depths in order to regulate the ink flow.

In the printing operation, the gravure plate rotates in a bath of ink, which fills the wells. Before reaching the paper, however, a "doctor blade" scrapes off the excess ink from the plate surface, leaving only the ink in the recessed wells.

The elaborate preparation in etching a gravure cylinder makes this a costly printing process. In order to justify the cost, a large print order—upward of 500,000 impressions—is needed. Once the plates have been made, high-speed, roll-fed gravure, commonly called rotogravure, can justify the expense.

Sheet-fed gravure printing also exists. The press runs are comparatively short compared with rotogravure, but the reproduction is of exceptionally high quality. The rich flow of ink gives illustrations the appearance of being three-dimensional. Try sheet-fed gravure for quality, but never for economy.

Choosing a Printing Process

Now that all three major printing processes have been surveyed, how do you know which to use? As yet, you do not have enough information to make that decision. These descriptions simply provide a background to supplement or give a base to your knowledge of printing. Reread them at various times during your graphic-arts education; each perusal will add more meaning to the learning process.

For now, we will endeavor to be practical and to enhance this knowledge with specific problems. The printing process chosen will depend, generally speaking, on the length of the press run, the paper used, the number of colors required, and perhaps even the typesetting, binding, and finishing requirements.

Problem 1. An advertising promotion brochure printed in runs of 100, 10,000, 100,000, or 1 million copies. The finished size is 8½ by 11 inches, with printing on both sides of the paper.

Answer 1a. For 100 copies: if only type is to be reproduced, you might consider a photocopying method. If the copy has to be backed up with graphics, the job lends itself to a quick-copy offset printing process. In rare cases, you might set hot type and print letterpress.

Answer 1b. For 10,000 copies: if you have to set hot-metal type, letterpress is possible, but doubtful. For one thing, if illustrations are used, letterpress requires making photoengravings. Lithography, on the other hand, will print both sides of the sheet at one time in what is called a "work-and-turn" form (see figure 2–2).

Answer 1c. For 100,000 copies: this sounds like a big run, but not when you step it up as you would in sheet-fed lithography. This is also a nice-size press run for a small web-offset press, which would feed a small roll and run at high speeds.

If you choose the sheet-fed method, try a larger press and print multiples. Study figure 2–3, which shows eight units up on a 23-by-35-inch press. Since eight pages are printed at one time, only an eighth

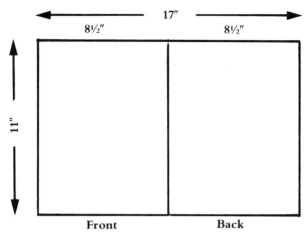

Figure 2-2. Design of a simple, two-page work-and-turn form. After printing one side, the sheet is turned, like the pages of a book, and backed up with the same printing plate. In this manner, the back page prints behind the front page, and vice versa.

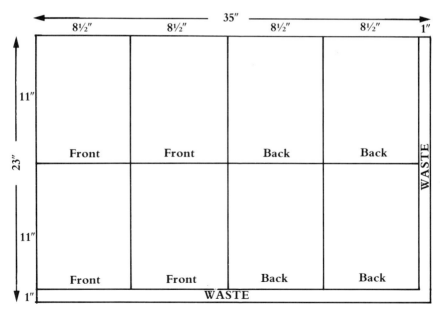

Figure 2-3. Diagram showing four front and four back pages up on a 23- by 35-inch sheet. This work-and-turn form is the same, in principle, as the one described in Figure 2-2.

of the paper is needed for each page, or 13,000 sheets (including spoilage allowance). After printing, the pages would be cut apart by a guillotine (straight-knife) cutter.

Answer 1d. For 1 million copies: this could be the time to use a rotary letterpress; try getting quotations from printers, if you wish. But considering the use of multiple press units, web offset offers the most flexibility. Regarding gravure: even though you are in the 1 million range, when you divide by eight, the press run is still too small to justify the relatively high cost.

Problem 2. A 128-page book printed in runs of 1,000, 10,000, or 100,000 copies. The finished page size is 5½ by 8½ inches.

Answer 2a. For 1,000 copies: as an exercise, how many sheets of paper would you say are needed here? Did you first think 128,000 sheets? Think again. Remember that one sheet of paper, printed on both sides, accounts for *two* pages; thus, only 64,000 sheets of paper are needed for the 1,000-copy print run.

Would you print this book by letterpress? Perhaps, since there is a lot of composition involved, and type has to be set. Illustrations might present a problem, however, since in letterpress, photos should be printed on a smooth, coated sheet of paper.

Another consideration: books are often reprinted when sales are unexpectedly high. With letterpress, the physical weight and bulk of the lead type and photoengravings might create handling and storage problems. Lithography, therefore, offers a better solution, since storage of the film negatives used for printing requires relatively little space.

Answer 2b. For 10,000 copies: the same reasoning applies here as in answer 2a above, and so lithography is still the best solution. Furthermore, lithography enables illustrations and photos to be reproduced on any paper that is sized for offset printing. Such paper is easy to obtain; the process is so popular that both coated and uncoated stock are standard purchase items. Considering the short press run, gravure is out of the question. •

From the paper standpoint, 640,000 sheets sounds tremendous, but figures can distort the situation. Using a 23-by-35-inch press, for example, it is relatively simple to print 16 pages on one side of the sheet (see figure 2–4). This produces a 32-page signature for binding purposes, which is normal.

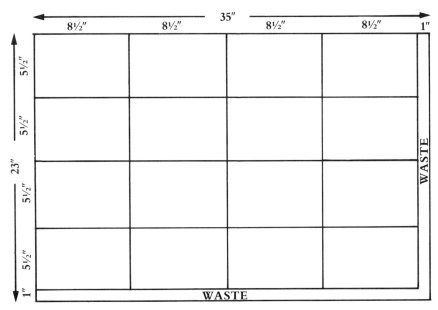

Figure 2-4. Layout of one side of a sheet, 16 pages up for printing, 32 pages when backed up.

Answer 2c. For 100,000 copies: the same reasoning again holds true for this situation. Letterpress is a possibility, and with the quantity involved, a web (or rotary) press is the best answer. Rotary letter-press, however, involves page makeup and electrotyping the pages. Another drawback might be the fact that coated paper would be required if photos are to be reproduced.

On the other hand, web offset fits all criteria: paper, plates, press-work, and delivering folded signatures for the bookbinding process. Again considering reprints, storing negatives for offset is routine and requires little space.

The rotogravure process is an unlikely candidate for these circum-stances, even though 64 million sheets of 5½-by-8½-inch paper are involved. For one thing, rotogravure paper must accept fluid ink, requiring more expensive coated paper.

Problem 3. Fifteen different greeting cards printed in runs of 20,000 copies each. Each greeting card is 5 by 7 inches when opened but is folded once to a finished size of 3½ by 5 inches. Two colors are to be printed on the outside; the inside is black ink.

Answer 3. Sheet-fed offset would be the best solution. The nearest standard-size sheet of paper would be 23 by 29 inches. Assuming that an 80-pound, fancy-finish, textured sheet would be used, check with a paper distributor for the exact types of paper available in that size.

Considering the color requirements, three printing plates would be necessary. The front page would be printed in two colors, requiring two printing plates (assuming that the same two colors are used on each of the 15 cards). Otherwise, more printing plates and printing impressions would be required. In any case, the third plate would print the backup of each card in black ink.

Since the job requires a textured sheet, letterpress is the wrong process, as it requires a smooth, coated sheet for best results.

Without going into great detail, it is interesting to note that with the same amount of paper, 16 cards can be printed at no extra cost.

Problem 4. A newsletter printed on newsprint paper at a run of 15,000 copies.

Answer 4. This situation presents another problem: newsprint. Letterpress and hot type are possibilities, but considering the increasing use of computerized cold type, a web-offset press is the best solution. Sheet-fed offset must be ruled out because newsprint typically comes in rolls. And once again, letterpress has restrictions. Because of the coarseness of newsprint, heavy type or solid illustrations would cause problems.

If it seems as though there is a bias against letterpress printing in this section, read chapter 4 to see exactly where this process fits in the industry. Large-run publications, for instance, have found rotary letterpress very useful, but they use a coated paper. Also, die-cutting, imprinting, and other specialty operations require the use of letterpress. Otherwise, most printing requirements are more suited to offset.

David Saltman

How to Use 3 *Lithographic Printing*

Lithography, also known today as offset lithography or simply offset, is based on the age-old principle that grease and water do not mix. The term *offset* refers to the fact that a printing plate containing the image to be reproduced offsets its printing area onto a blanket, which, in turn, offsets its image onto paper.

Lithography, which means "writing by stone," was invented in 1798 by the German graphic artist Alois Senefelder. A fictionalized account of the incident recalls Senefelder using a greasy crayon to write his mother's laundry list on a freshly polished slab of stone. The curious Senefelder then discovered that the crayon images, when treated with chemicals and ink, could be transferred onto paper. There are less-romantic accounts of the invention, but they all lead back to grease versus water. Furthermore, Senefelder found that copper or zinc plates could be used as well as stone, and he eventually invented a press that automatically dampened and inked the plates.

Modern offset lithography, today's most prolific printing process, is based largely on the principles of photography. In order to make the printing plate, all the graphic material—type, line art, photographs, and so on—are photographed. The final, one-piece printing plate is made to fit the size of the press. A brief description of platemaking follows, to help you further understand the process.

Platemaking

First, the individual graphic components are photographed separately. Then they are positioned or stripped onto a piece of goldenrod paper, glass, or vinyl to produce a flat. Adhesive tape holds the film in place. Pinholes, dirt marks, cut lines, and other extraneous marks are blocked out or opaqued on the flat so that when exposed to light they will not appear on the printing image. Conversely, all the remaining matter on the flat will permit the passage of light and thus transfer the image on the film to the printing plate.

After the film has been stripped into position and opaqued, the flat is placed onto a sensitized metal sheet—the plate—and then sealed in a vacuum frame. The plate, usually made of aluminum, is coated with a thin film of light-sensitive material. The vacuum removes all the air so as to ensure perfect contact between the flat and the plate. Strong light then penetrates the flat and transfers the printing area onto the plate. After the light exposure, the plate is developed to make the image areas ink-receptive; then it is treated to make the nonimage areas water-receptive (see figure 3–1). The next step, *proofing,* checks for accuracy.

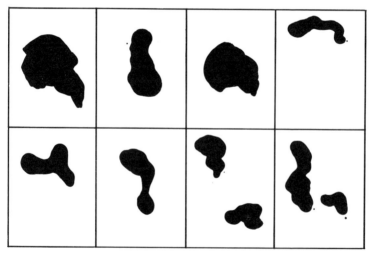

Figure 3-1. A typical lithographic flat ready for exposure onto a printing plate. A stripper will use a razor blade to open up the image by cutting away unwanted portions of the flat. Images shown as small openings on a page may also have a color flat to print in register with a basic "black" flat.

Proofing

Proofing the flats catches errors and mistakes before they appear on the final printing plate. Most printers supply proofs to their customers so that they can check the accuracy of layouts, the position of graphic elements, the register of multiple plates (required when printing in two or more colors), or just see what the job will look like before it goes to press.

Generally, a photochemical process is used for making proofs of single- and multicolor work. Several types of material are used in the process, but the most accurate and commonly used is a brownprint paper known by a variety of names including vandyke, Solar, and silver print. (In some cases, such as with print ads, proofs are referred to as "blues.")

Brownprint paper is used to make positive proofs from negative flats. The paper and stripped flats are exposed together in a vacuum-printing frame to arc lights. The exposed brownprint is then developed and dried. Now it is ready to send to the customer for any corrections before the final platemaking.

Preparing Type and Art

Any printed piece is made up of two essential elements—type and various kinds of illustrations—and both must be prepared for the printing process. (Typography is covered in chapter 9, and preparing artwork and mechanical art are covered in chapters 8 and 10, respectively, but for the purpose here of describing lithography, we will briefly touch on the preparation of type and illustrations.)

The rise of lithography has prompted methods for converting three-dimensional ("hot") metal type into two-dimensional ("cold") type. But this is often unnecessary, as phototypesetting systems are predominantly used today, and computerized typesetting is rapidly becoming the industry standard. Once the type is set, it is combined with any illustrated material and prepared for the platemaking process.

Preparing line art—art that contains no shades of gray and prints in a solid color or black—is similar to preparing type. Indeed, line art can be stripped onto the same flat with the type. Photographs, however, are another matter and require a different preparation process.

Photographs are composed of continuous tones of gray, referred to as highlights, middletones, or dark tones. The only way a photograph can be reproduced in any printing process is to convert the photograph into a series of evenly spaced dots of varying sizes and shapes. The result is a halftone. Once on press, smaller dots accept less ink and larger dots accept more ink, thus creating the appearance of lighter and darker images. In effect, the eye perceives an optical illusion, a shade of gray. For example, if a halftone dot in a square covers 40 percent of the square, the other 60 percent is white space (see figure 3-2).

A halftone is produced by placing a highly fine-lined halftone screen between a camera lens and photographic film. Light reflected from the original photograph then passes through the screen openings. Since dark areas reflect less light and light areas reflect more light, the result is an uneven pattern of dots—a halftone (see figure 3–3).

There are two methods of printing two-color halftones (known as duotones), using either a color tint or a second, color negative. Full-color copy, however, must be color separated; it is reproduced with three partially transparent inks, referred to as process inks, plus black. The three process colors are cyan, yellow, and magenta. In turn, four negatives are needed for making the printing plates required for printing the separate colors. Nowadays, the most popular method

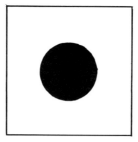

Figure 3-2. The printing block covers 40 percent of the unit size, with the balance appearing as white space. The eye interprets the dot and surrounding white space as a tone of gray. If the screen is 150 spaces to the linear inch, the unit size will be 1/150th of a square inch. In one square-inch area, therefore, 150 × 150 = 22,500 dots per square inch.

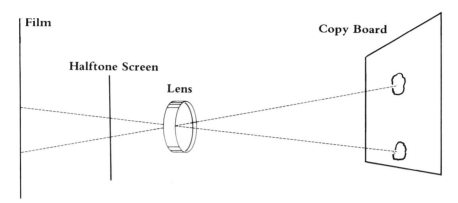

Figure 3-3. Reflected light from the photograph passes through a halftone screen, positioned between the camera lens and the photographic film. This breaks up the image into a pattern of varying-sized dots, depending on the amount of light reflected from the tone values of the photograph.

of color separation is electronic scanning. The separate negatives are proofed, color-corrected if necessary, and placed in register with one another. (For more on preparing artwork, see chapter 8.) Finally, all the graphic elements are assembled into a layout design, and the mechanical art is prepared (as described in chapter 10). Now the job is ready for the platemaking process.

Lithographic Presswork

Lithographic offset presses come in a variety of makes and models, but they are generally differentiated by (1) the size of the paper that can pass through the press; (2) the number of different colors (or units) a press can print; (3) whether it handles single sheets or rolls (webs) of paper; and (4) whether it is a perfecting machine, which means that it can print on both sides of the paper in one pass through the press.

With any type of press, the printing process centers around the three cylinders of the printing unit: the plate cylinder, the blanket cylinder, and the impression cylinder. Following the grease-versus-water axiom again, set against the plate cylinder is an inking system and a dampening system. The sheet-fed offset press illustrates the process.

Sheet-fed Offset Presses

In the sheet-fed press, the printing plate is attached to the plate cylinder. As the plate cylinder revolves counterclockwise, the dampening (water) system passes over the plate, and the nonimage areas accept the moisture. The greasy image areas repel the moisture but accept the ink from the inking system's rollers that follow. The plate cylinder then transfers the inked images to the revolving blanket cylinder. The paper is drawn around the impression cylinder and brought into contact with the inked blanket cylinder, and the image is transferred to the paper (see figure 3-4). The printing cycle is now complete, and the sheet continues to the delivery end of the press. This describes the operation of a single-color or single-unit press.

The process alters a bit with the multicolor sheet-fed press. The separate plates for each of the four colors are positioned onto the individual press units. When the press begins running, the paper passes

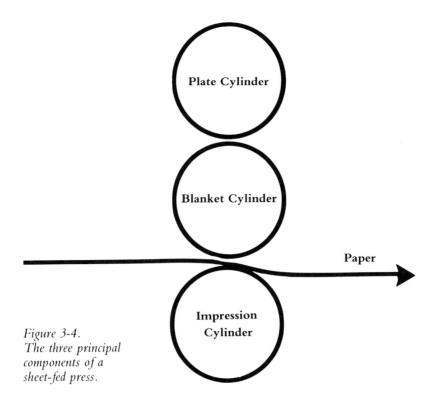

Figure 3-4.
The three principal
components of a
sheet-fed press.

through each press unit, as described above, and accepts the ink from each one. Generally, one unit contains black ink, while each succeeding unit contains the three other process-color inks.

Multicolor presses generally contain two or four press units. However, it is possible to print colored ink on a single-color press. The paper passes through the press once for each color. In order to print on the back of the sheet, the paper is turned over and the cycle is repeated.

Web-Offset Presses

The more interesting types of lithographic printing are being produced today on web-offset presses. Although such presses are made in special sizes, the most popular is the commercial web-offset press, which can run a 16-page, 8½-by-11-inch trimmed-size signature. Its cutoff dimension is about 22¾ inches, and across the cylinder the sizes range from 35 to 38 inches. The next-most-popular web-offset press is half that size and is referred to as a half-web or miniweb. Smaller web-offset presses are also used to print, for example, snap-out business forms.

The operation of the web-offset press is similar to that of the sheet-fed press, except that rolls of paper are handled instead of sheets. The principles and operations of cylinder pressures, plate handling, blankets, inking, dampening, and so on are practically identical. However, the web-offset is a perfecting machine.

To help you understand the capabilities and limitations of web-offset presses, refer to the diagrams in figures 3–5a and 3–5b while this discussion continues.

In example A, notice the roll of paper passing through four units of a web press while the second roll of paper is idle. This is because the job calls for four-color printing on both sides of the paper, and all the press units are used in the printing operation.

In example B, two rolls of paper are used at the same time, each printing two colors on both sides of the web. While the second roll starts with the third press unit, both units are synchronized so that they come together at the delivery end and fold as a single signature.

Some web-offset presses have six units so that one roll can print four colors, the second can print two colors, and both rolls can be folded together as one signature.

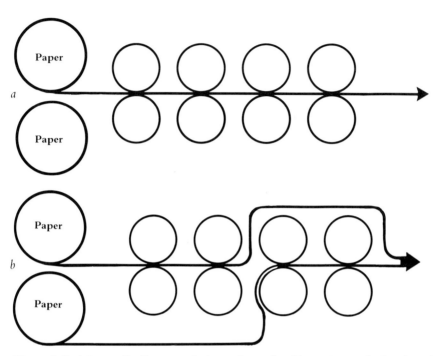

Figure 3-5. (a): a roll of paper printing a four-color illustration on both sides of the web. Since all units are used in printing four colors, a second web cannot be used unless more press units are added. (b): a roll of paper prints two colors on two units, bypassing the remaining units. The second roll is fed through the third and fourth units, also printing two colors on both sides of the web. At the delivery end, both webs merge to form a single signature for binding.

Perhaps you are wondering what happened to the impression cylinders on the web-offset press shown in figure 3–5a. The answer: there aren't any. This is known as a blanket-to-blanket web-offset press. Look at the illustration again and notice how the paper passes between the two blanket cylinders. (The plate cylinders are not shown.) As each printing plate transfers its image to the blanket cylinder, each blanket acts as an impression cylinder for its counterpart. As the paper passes through each pair of blanket cylinders, it is perfected or printed simultaneously on both sides of the paper.

Color Flexibility
To further stimulate your thinking about web-offset, refer again to figure 3–5b. In this example, assume that you plan to print red and

black on the first two sets of cylinders. On the third and fourth cylinders, by feeding a second roll of paper, you can select any colors you wish. Thus, the first two sets of press units will print red and black on both sides of the paper, but the next roll will print red and green. However, if you want to get a lot of color out of this press run, carefully consider the following.

Assume that black ink is basic for text matter. Therefore, we will run black ink on the top and bottom of units one and three. On the top of the second unit, we will run red ink, and on the bottom part, blue ink. On press unit four, it will be green ink on the top side of the paper and brown ink on the bottom side. Now, let us consider the result.

On a two-color web run, we have printed black, red, blue, green, and brown at no additional cost. This type of presswork could add a lot of spice to, say, a product catalog; for this maximum of color you only pay the regular cost of running a four-unit web press. Incidentally, to avoid confusion when talking to a printer, refer to this type of web-offset press as "four over four," rather than confusing it with an eight-unit press.

Web-Offset Pros and Cons

Following are advantages and disadvantages to printing on a web-offset press:

Advantages

• Paper is cheaper in rolls than in sheets.

• The speed of the web press is much greater than that of a sheet-fed press.

• The web press is perfecting.

• Paper can be folded into signatures at the delivery end of the press; this provides sizable time and cost savings in the bindery operations.

• Web presses can have the flexibility of delivering in sheets as well as folding. The size, once again, is limited by the cylinder circumference for cutoff.

• The web is essential for long press-runs.

• Recently there have been many adaptations at the delivery end of the press that offer considerable savings by bypassing the bindery. Two such examples involve special folds and gluing; be sure to ask your printer for information.

Disadvantages
• The width of the paper roll can be varied within maximum and minimum sizes, but the web cutoff is limited by the circumference of the cutoff cylinder.
• Paper spoilage is much higher than with sheet-fed presses (generally about twice as much).

Heat–Set and Non–Heat-Set Web Presses

The heat-set web press has an oven attached to it so that coated paper, for example, passes through a heating element after printing to accelerate the ink drying. Since the press is more expensive, the impressions purchased on this press would in turn be more expensive. This type of press is necessary for coated stock and is desirable for high-quality printing.

The non–heat-set press has no drying oven and is, therefore, sold at a lower press-time rate. This type of press is ideal for newspaper printing or for uncoated stock that does not require an oven to assist in the ink drying.

Step and Repeat

The step-and-repeat process is one of the great advantages of lithography. By this means, a single image can be multiplied, or "stepped up," on a printing plate in perfect register in black-and-white or color process. When multiple images are required, extra negatives can quickly and easily be made. Then, by stripping them in position, an extra exposure reproduces the same image as often as necessary. Upon completion, the job can be cut apart at the bindery. The process can be a very economical one.

For this purpose, a step-and-repeat camera is the best answer. The machine is very accurate in stepping horizontally, vertically, or both. For example, consider a job that requires the reproduction of 10 million labels for a cosmetic product, printed in one, two, or four colors. By preparing just one image, this can be stepped up on the printing plate any number of times to fit the requirements. Assuming that this is done 96 units up, for example, little more than 100,000 impressions are required to print the job. If in multiple colors, it can also be done on a multicolor press.

Now some practical problems and solutions involving lithographic offset printing will be considered.

Cover Stock Cutouts

Problem 1. An 8½-by-11-inch promotional piece is to be printed on cover stock in two colors. The press run will be 20,000 copies. What are the most economical alternatives?

Discussion. A standard cover-stock size is 20 by 26 inches, but often some specialty covers come in only 26 by 40 inches. Here we will refer to the latter size, since it is more flexible.

Answer 1a. Returning to figure 3–6a, we have eight units out, with 4 inches of waste at the bottom and 6 inches of waste along the side. Dividing 20,000 by eight units, we need 2,500 sheets, printed in two colors on both sides. Allowing for spoilage, order 3,000 sheets.

Answer 1b. This solution is more effective, since we work with the dimensions differently: we get three units out of the 26-inch dimension, and three units of 11 inches the opposite way (see figure 3–6b). Now divide 20,000 by 9 to get a figure of 2,222, roughly. Allowing for spoilage, and rounding to the nearest even number, place an order for 2,750 sheets.

Answer 1c. We improved our paper utilization, but there is still a better solution. In figure 3–6c, we have squeezed 10 units out of the sheet by altering the dimension both ways. Each new solution shrinks paper waste, which becomes considerable with expensive cover stock. In this case, the need is for 2,000 sheets, plus spoilage, or 2,500 sheets.

Not only have we saved paper in each case but we have also reduced printing impressions. The reduction in impressions is equal to the paper-saving figure multiplied by four. This represents two colors on each side of the sheet.

We must also consider other factors: first, there are two grain directions of paper. This may not be important in some cases but may prove to be prohibitively expensive in others. Secondly, it is most important to position the paper in such a manner that it can be cut by a guillotine (straight-knife) cutter. This can be done with a straight cut near the center of the paper, between the 8½- and 11-inch horizontal dimensions.

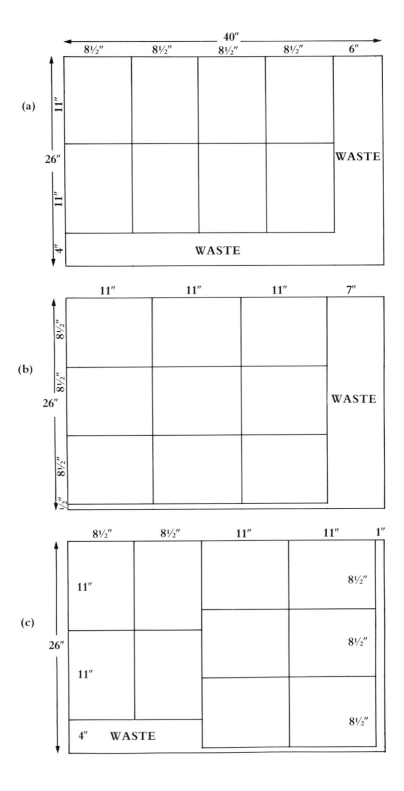

Twenty-four-page Signature

Here is an interesting problem that can be worked out on a web-offset press.

Problem 2. The job calls for the printing of a 24-page saddle-stitch booklet, in two colors, with two sides printed on 50-pound offset stock. The print run is 100,000 copies, and the finished size is 8½ by 10⅞ inches.

Answer 2. As web signatures go, we are tempted to think of a 16-page signature and an 8-page signature printed on a 36-inch web press. This would involve printing and gathering two separate signatures for binding, before stitching. A better solution is to feed a web and a half-web through the press, with both coming together at the delivery end. This becomes one 24-page signature for stitching (see figure 3–7).

Note that we used a 35-inch roll width to accommodate the trim to 8½ inches after stitching. The 17½-inch roll is obtained by slitting 35-inch rolls in two. Regarding the 10⅞-inch dimension, there is no flexibility in this case, since the manufacturing design of the press calls for a fixed cutoff of 22¾ inches.

Perhaps you are wondering why an 11-inch dimension was not specified. This is possible on some presses with a larger cutoff. After printing in the web operation, the paper is caught by pin projections, which grab the paper and hold it taut. During the folding operation, the roll rotates and gets chopped by a knife blade, severing it from the main paper roll. The paper is delivered as a folded signature. At the bindery, the section showing the pinholes is trimmed off as part of the stitching and trimming operation. For an example, take a look at your local newspaper, which is probably printed by web-offset. Notice the pinholes on half the paper. These are not trimmed off in a newspaper operation since there is no stitching and, therefore, no need to add extra binding expenses.

Figure 3-6. (a): eight sheets of 8½- by-11-inch cover stock are cut out of the 26-by-40-inch size. Note the waste on the bottom and side. (b): nine sheets cut out of the same 26- by-40-inch cover stock by changing the dimensions. The waste is less than in figure a. (c): ten sheets can be cut out of the 26- by-40-inch cover stock with "crossed grains."

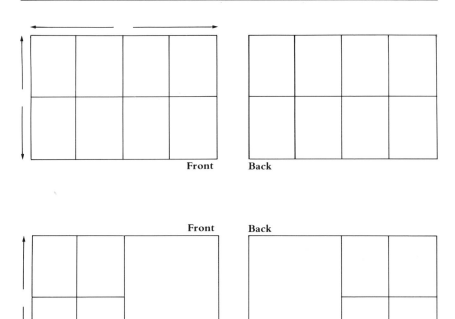

Front   Back

Front   Back

Figure 3-7. The top section shows the front and back of a 16-page web, while the bottom section shows the front and back of an 8-page half web. At the delivery end, both forms combine to form a 24-page signature, ready for binding.

Problem 3. This is the same as Problem 2, except the job calls for a 56-page booklet.

Answer 3. Much of the solution has been discussed in the previous example. Use two full paper webs to form a 32-page signature. Gather both webs to complete the necessary 56 pages. If the book is to have a cover, this can be printed in multiples by using the step-and-repeat system and running the job on a sheet-fed offset press. The cover is then gathered on the outside—a wrap-around—as an additional four-page signature.

How to Use 4
Letterpress Printing

Letterpress printing—or printing from a relief surface—is alive and well. Although specialized, short-run letterpress work is produced at relatively low speeds, current technology also allows some high-speed letterpress printing. Overall, letterpress is a versatile and useful method for printing products that might otherwise be impossible to produce.

The Letterpress Printing Method

The letterpress process is based on type or printing plates that contain images that stand out in relief. The basic principle is illustrated in figure 4–1. The type character stands up in relief from its base, and a piece of paper is displayed that has been imaged from the type after it has been inked. Both the type and paper must be pressed together so the image will actually transfer. Nearly any material can be printed by this method, assuming that the type character and the substrate (commonly paper) conform to one another and there is even pressure between both to cause the ink to transfer.

Varieties of metal type, such as Linotype and Intertype slugs, have been and continue to be used to print images by the letterpress method. Individual characters of metal type, either that of foundry type or Monotype, also continue to be used. The metal typeform shown in figure 4–2 is typical of those used to print the return address of companies or individuals on business envelopes. (Refer to chapter 9 for more information on type.)

Metal and plastic plates are also frequently used to print products

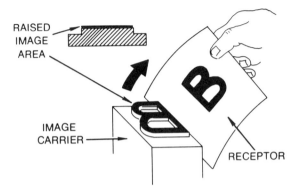

Figure 4-1. The basic principle of transferring relief images, as used in letterpress printing.

Figure 4-2. An example of letterpress type slugs that have been cast from molten metal.

from relief surfaces. This type of plate is much easier to prepare than a metal plate. Moreover, the cost is lower, while the reproduction quality is as good as or better than that obtained by using any one of several kinds of metal plates.

Flexography is another form of letterpress printing. Instead of metal printing plates, flexible rubber or plastic plates are used to reproduce the image. The ink is also more liquid than regular letterpress ink, which has a pasty consistency. Printing presses have been engineered to utilize these flexible plates and along with their thin ink to print products such as packaging materials made of transparent film, food cartons, paper bags, business forms, envelopes, and milk cartons. (For more information on flexography, consult chapter 7.)

History of Letterpress Printing

Printing dates back to the year 2000 B.C., when the Babylonians printed playing cards. Ancient Chinese and Japanese printers used carved wooden blocks to transfer images onto paper. It was not until the early 1400s that Europeans invented a mechanical form of block printing. Still, all the work involved—such as carving the wooden blocks and transferring the inked images to dampened, handmade paper—made this a slow process for the skilled artisans who pioneered this new craft.

The major problem with using wooden blocks was that a completely new carving had to be made for each image. Moreover, none of the illustrations or readable typefaces could be reused, because the entire relief image was in one piece.

It took the lifelong efforts of Johann Gutenberg of Mainz, Germany, to solve the mystery of movable metal type in 1450. He knew there had to be a simpler way of creating a type page and then reusing some or all of the type for another page. His first major work, the "Bible of 42 Lines" (referring to the number of lines per page), was released to the world in 1456. Nearly 200 copies of the 1,300-page Bible were printed, and a few copies still exist, one of which is in the National Archives in Washington, D.C.

Following Gutenberg's momentous invention and its subsequent development, printing spread rapidly throughout the civilized world. Up until that time, remember, all books had been reproduced completely by hand. Scribes and monks spent months and sometimes years hand printing even one copy of a religious book, most often the Bible.

Gutenberg is also responsible for developing the printing press. He converted a wine press into a manually operated machine equipped with a device that held the typeform and paper in their proper positions. Once these important ingredients were ready, ink was spread over the raised letters of the typeform. The flat surface, called a *platen,* was then slowly lowered, pressing well-moistened paper against the relief surface. The ink was transferred onto the paper, and another duplicate image was produced.

Letterpress Printing Presses

Since the time of Gutenberg, a large number of printing presses have been designed to reproduce images from relief type and plates. All different kinds of printing presses, suitable for any of the printing processes, fall into one of three categories, each with a given capacity and predilection for certain types of printing work: platen, cylinder, and rotary, illustrated in figure 4–3. All three designs can be used for letterpress printing.

The *platen press* uses a clamshell motion to carry the platen, which holds the paper, up against the relief printing form. On early models, the press operator used a foot pedal to operate the press; his hands fed and removed the paper. Many of today's platens are automatic, and they are currently being manufactured and operated throughout the world. Although they are generally slower than the other two press designs, platens are used to produce small-quantity, high-quality work.

The *cylinder press,* like the platen, has a flat typeform, but it utilizes a large, round cylinder to hold the paper in place and roll it against the relief images of type, illustrations, and halftone photographs. Since the cylinder touches only a small part of the type at any given time, the pressure is uniform, resulting in excellent printing quality.

Both platen and cylinder presses use individual sheets of paper, a factor that limits their speed. This restriction was overcome with the development of the *rotary press,* which feeds off an endless roll, or web, of paper (hence the term *web press*). Modern, high-speed rotary presses cut a continuous roll of printed paper into sheets and fold them into pages. This once made them essential to large-circulation

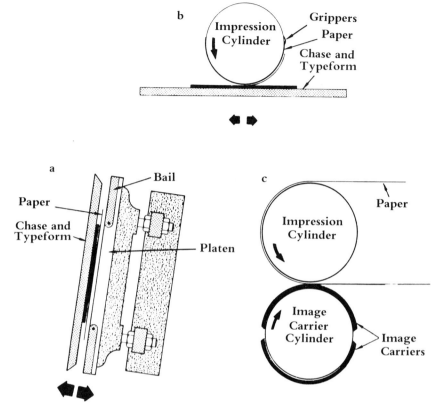

Figure 4-3. The three printing press designs: (a) platen; (b) cylinder; and (c) rotary.

newspaper printing, yet most dailies have since converted their operations to offset lithography.

Preparing Halftones for Letterpress

Printing halftone photographs on letterpress equipment has not been common—or recommended—since the advancement of lithography, and so this process is limited mostly to those daily and weekly newspapers that still print on letterpress equipment.

To produce a halftone for letterpress—a time-consuming and expensive process—a relief printing plate is made. First, a halftone negative is made from the original black-and-white photograph. A halftone screen breaks the image down into a series of dots that represent the gray tones of the photo. Next, a relief plate is made from zinc, copper, magnesium, or a photopolymer. The negative is placed on the metal or photopolymer surface, exposed to bright light, and the nonimage material is washed away. This leaves the dots forming the halftone image standing in relief. (This process is similar to plate-making in lithography, as described in chapter 3.)

Coarse halftone screens, from 65 to 100 lines per inch, are typically used for letterpress. This is because very fine halftone dots may not be able to withstand the pressure associated with letterpress printing; conversely, larger dots tend to fill in with ink and spread on the paper. Therefore, it is advisable to use halftones sparingly in letter-press printing. In any case, ask the printer for several printed samples before making your decision.

Products of Letterpress Printing

According to a 1981 report, "Status of Printing in the U.S.A.," by 1985 letterpress will be used to print approximately 12 percent of most printed products. The figure was 20 percent in 1981. Letterpress will continue to decrease in use as other printing processes erode its market. By 1990, the figure will drop to about 5 percent.

Even so, letterpress is still widely used in the label, packaging, and business-forms segments of the printing industry. Its characteristically heavy and uniform deposits of ink, especially in multicolor work, keep letterpress strong in these areas. Letterpress is also used for short-run publications because of its relatively low preparation and operating costs.

Commercial printers' use of letterpress is limited, but certain specialty items are best printed from relief images. Short-run work, such as printing business cards, letterheads, and envelopes, takes best advantage of letterpress. Hot type from Linotype or Intertype machines can be inexpensively prepared in minutes, and the job can be printed on an automatic platen press (see figure 4–4).

Imprinting, whereby personalized information is added to a pre-printed publication or advertising flier, is another use for letterpress printing. For example, a national corporation may print an advertising publication of its products but leave space on the cover so local distributors can print their names and addresses. This type of job can also be handled by automatic platen presses.

Figure 4-4. A platen letterpress, specially designed for imprinting, automatically feeds and delivers the printed sheet of paper. (Courtesy of Heidelberg, USA)

Also well suited to the letterpress method are wedding invitations, tickets for local events, invoice and billing slips, and other business forms, along with certain bulky or awkward items, such as a lectern Bible or reproduction art pieces.

Certain specialty products require specially designed letterpress equipment to perform finishing techniques such as perforating, scoring (creasing), hot stamping, embossing, and die-cutting (see chapter 14).

Figure 4-5. A platen letterpress outfitted with a heating element and a roll-feed for foil stamping. (Courtesy of Heidelberg, USA)

Hot stamping, sometimes called foil printing, is done on a machine. The machine uses raised type to press the images onto the product. Special nonmelting foundry-type Linotype slugs and metal engravings must be used so they can be heated and then pressed against the product. Gold, silver, or colored foils are placed between the hot raised images and the product. The images are transferred by combining just the right amount of heat and pressure.

Automatic platen presses have been equipped with special heating coils to prepare the typeform and feeding mechanisms for the foil

(see figure 4–5). Such machinery allows specialty products to be imaged at a faster rate than on conventional letterpress equipment.

For ease in tearing a card from an advertising flier or folding a
printed card, letterpress platen presses are used to perforate and score
the printed products. These techniques can be performed on web-
rotary presses directly during the printing process, but short-run work
can best be done on a platen or cylinder letterpress. A platen press
is also very useful for embossing and die-cutting, especially for short
runs.

Numbering is another task best accomplished by using either a
platen or cylinder press. A numbering machine, as shown in figure
4–6, is an intricate device that requires ink and pressure to transfer
the needed numbers one after another onto the product.

To apply bar codes to such products as manufactured forms, bills
of lading, envelopes, and bags, the letterpress relief-printing process
should be used. The bar-code head, as shown in figure 4–7, transfers

*Figure 4-6. A numbering machine can be attached to a letterpress. Each time the
plunger imprinted with "No." is pressed, the next digit will revolve for the next
impression. (Courtesy of Leibinger-Roberts, Inc.)*

Figure 4-7. A triple bar-code head, attached to a letterpress, prints identification codes on a variety of products. (Courtesy of Leibinger-Roberts, Inc.)

the needed code to the product. In some situations, numbering machines and bar-code heads are both successfully attached to the delivery portion of a sheet-fed lithographic press. The imaging, though, is still accomplished via the relief printing process.

Paper and Ink Needs

When letterpress was the primary printing process, paper was specially formulated and manufactured for relief printing. When other processes, such as lithography and gravure, became popular, paper qualities and grades had to be changed to meet the differing needs.

In general, papers used in letterpress printing should have a smooth, flat surface and be of uniform thickness. Coated papers generally work well, but uncoated stock can also be used successfully. As noted earlier in this chapter, line copy is now the predominant type of material printed with letterpress. So if halftone engravings are to be used, it will be necessary to use a smooth, coated paper stock, especially if fine detail is required.

Paper for letterpress printing should have good opacity. It should be able to withstand heavy pressure; the paper surface needs to bounce back to its original position and not remain compressed. This is especially true if printing is to occur on both sides of the paper.

It may be possible to use a less-expensive paper for letterpress than for lithography or gravure. Because only the image areas contact the paper surface, there is less stress placed on the paper surface coating than in lithography. The lithographic blanket cylinder, for instance, contacts the entire surface of the paper and causes considerable stress due to both pressure and lifting or tearing the paper apart.

Today, paper manufacturers have formulated their many products with such precision and quality that most varieties can be printed on by letterpress or lithography. There are limitations, though, so again a designer or planner of printing should discuss paper requirements and needs with a printer before progressing too far into the design and layout stages. (Also, see chapter 11 for information on selecting paper.)

It is not necessary, however, to be acquainted with the chemistry of printing ink. The responsibility lies with the printer to know ink properties and how an ink will behave on a given paper stock. Select the paper, and then ask the printer which kinds and colors of inks are suitable for that paper. The proper color or colors can then be determined and selected with confidence.

Planning and Producing a Letterpress Job

It is important to keep several points in mind when planning and designing a product that will be printed via letterpress:

1. Plan jobs with most if not all of the printed content in the form of type and line illustrations. Stay away from halftones as much as possible. A great deal of cost is involved in producing a halftone engraving, and it generally takes longer for the press operators to set up and print halftones.

2. Use letterpress work for short runs, unless the printer still has a high-speed rotary press available. Even then, the run should be of suitable length, several thousand pieces at least, before the use of a rotary press is considered. When press runs are in the neighborhood of a few hundred to a few thousand pieces, it is probably most economical to consider letterpress.

3. Consider the availability of commercial printers who still have letterpress equipment. During the last decade, hundreds of com-

mercial printers sold or abandoned their letterpress equipment in favor of lithographic equipment. This has left a serious void, since some jobs are still best suited to relief printing, as noted earlier in this chapter.

If a job is to be bid on by several printers, it may be difficult to locate enough of them with letterpress equipment within a reasonable geographical area. This could cause transportation problems, especially if your timetable is tight. Of course, if there is sufficient lead time, the geographical distance between you and the printer is insignificant.

4. Finally, as discussed earlier, research the available inks and papers that are suitable for letterpress printing.

Once the design and layout work is finished, the letterpress printer can begin production. Linotype, Intertype, or possibly foundry type is set for the type. It is possible, using cold type, set by photographic or electronic methods, to incorporate line illustrations and halftones.

Figure 4-8. To correct a letterpress photopolymer printing plate, doubled-sided tape is used to hold the corrected information in place. (Courtesy BASF Systems Corp.)

Then these components are assembled into a camera-ready paste-up. A film negative is prepared, which is used to make a photopolymer relief plate. These high-quality plates can be made in a matter of minutes. It is also possible to make corrections on these plates, as shown in figure 4–8, and they can be used on each of the three styles of printing presses—platen, cylinder, or rotary. (For more information on preparing mechanical art, see chapter 8.)

Once the relief type or plates are made, the job is ready to be printed. Letterpress equipment generally operates more slowly than lithographic equipment does, but this usually causes few delays in completing the job on time. The type of work suitable for letterpress printing permits the equipment to be adjusted, and the run can then be completed with few if any stops. The finishing and binding phase of a letterpress job is much the same as with the other printing processes (see chapter 14).

Generally speaking, if your printing requirements call primarily for the reproduction of type (and no illustrations or halftones), and if the number of copies needed is relatively small, the best process may be letterpress. Notwithstanding this advice, your decision may also come down to a matter of economics and budgeting. So be sure to first consult with your printer about which printing method best suits your needs as well as your budget. (For more information on planning and budgeting, see chapter 12.)

How to Use 5
Gravure Printing

"The art of the armorer."

This rather romantic description reminds us of the beginnings of the third major printing method: intaglio. That word—pronounce it in-*tal*-yo in its original Italian, or anglicize it to in-*tag*-leo—means "incised." And that describes the type of printing plate used in this printing method, often referred to as gravure.

When knighthood was in flower, the armor worn and the weapons wielded were richly decorated with designs cut into the metal, each set ornamented extemporaneously and each unique. In order to record the design, so it could be duplicated when an original was damaged or lost on the field of battle, the armorer used a crude but adequate reproduction process.

A dark liquid was spread all over the surface of the armor. The liquid was carefully wiped off the raised surface but allowed to remain in the engraved ornamentation. Then a white cloth was smoothed onto the metal, the liquid in the crevices soaking into the fabric. The result was a "print" of the design on the cloth. The image was not very sharp, of course, as the "ink" feathered into the cloth, but it served its purpose. The method was especially useful because cloth was flexible and could wrap over curved areas—which is what most of the decorated surfaces of the weaponry were—the breastplate, handles of swords and maces, shafts of lances, and so on.

Simple logic expanded this intaglio method to flat plates printed on paper. The first identifiable commercial use was to reproduce illustrations in the form of a copperplate etching. Ultimately, it led to the curved plates and web-feeding that today we call rotogravure.

Copperplate Etching

The first true intaglio printing was that of copperplate etching. Many of the great Renaissance artists (most notably, perhaps, Rembrandt) made this a high art form. A look at this process enables us to understand easily the intaglio principle in practical application.

The artist coats a copper plate with an acid resist. He scratches through this coating to expose the copper and puts the plate in an acid bath. After the acid has eaten sufficiently into the copper, the plate is removed and washed in plain water. Then a second set of scratches exposes the plate, and again the acid etches the metal. The washing, scratching, and etching processes are repeated as many times as necessary. By the time the last lines have been etched, the first lines have been exposed several times to the acid and are much deeper. The variation in depth comes not from the density of the lines scratched into the resist ground but by the total time the metal is exposed to the acid.

The finished plate is now inked. Then, the printer, using either a cloth or, more frequently, the heel of his hand, wipes the surface of the plate clean, leaving the ink in the incisions. This requires great skill. Should the press operator wipe too gently, ink will remain on the surface and, of course, transfer onto the paper. Should the operator press too heavily, some of the ink will be forced out of the cavities, and the resulting printing image will be weak.

Paper, wetted to give it greater flexibility, is pressed onto the plate and, minutely, into the engraved lines. The ink is lifted out of the incisions by capillary action, and we have a printed page (see figure 5–1). It is interesting to note that the first picture of Gutenberg's letterpress was printed by intaglio during the period of incunabula, 1450–1500.

Rotogravure

As with other printing processes, photography was married to intaglio and became photogravure. Likewise, the rotary press, the halftone process, and process color were all combined into rotogravure. The resulting printing process is a mechanization of the printing of copperplate etchings.

The rotogravure printing plate is the only one made originally in a curved form. (Some gravure plates, like those for letterpress and

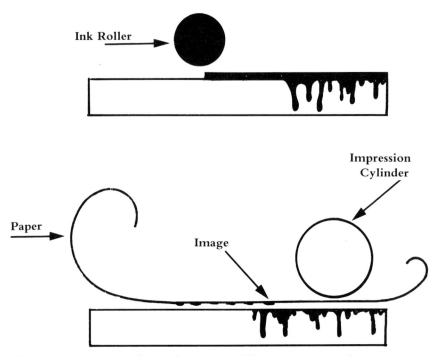

Figure 5-1. Schematic of sheet-fed gravure. This is the process of printing a copperplate etching and flat intaglio plates. In the top portion, the ink roller has deposited ink onto the face of the plate and into the incisions. In the lower sketch, the plate has been wiped clean, leaving ink only in the depressions. The impression cylinder presses the paper on the plate, and the ink, by capillary action, leaves the incisions and is deposited on the paper.

lithography, are made flat and then wrapped around a cylinder for rotary printing. By the stereotype process, flat relief forms are converted into cylindrical printing elements.) Rotogravure plates are cylinders of either solid copper or of iron, steel, or aluminum coated with copper.

Into the copper skin are incised millions of tiny wells of equal area but of varying depths. On the press, the plate is flooded with ink which, of course, also fills the wells. The surface is scraped clean by a doctor blade, really a scalpel-sharp piece of surgical steel. The paper web is pressed against the copper cylinder by a rubber-blanketed impression cylinder, the ink transfers onto the paper, and we have a printed image of high clarity (see figure 5–2).

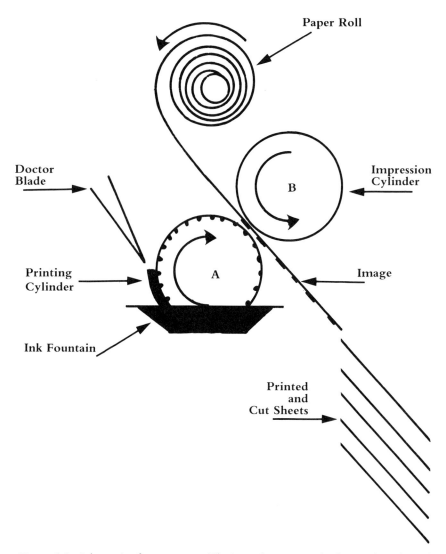

Figure 5-2. Schematic of rotogravure. The incised printing cylinder revolves through the ink fountain where both the surface and the incisions are covered with ink. The doctor blade scrapes the surface clean. Paper, feeding off a roll, is pressed by the impression cylinder on the printing plate. Ink leaves the incisions to create the printed image. At the end of the press, the paper web is cut into separate sheets and folded as necessary.

Several advantages are immediately apparent. The copper cylinder, which is ground down and replated for each job, is polished to a tolerance of a thousandth of an inch. Therefore, no makeready (a process that aligns the contact between printing elements and paper) is required, and the quality of the printed image does not greatly depend on the skill and care of the press operator in registering plates and packing the impression cylinder. The potential waste of not-yet-perfect early impressions is eliminated; every impression from first to last is identically true.

Rotogravure ink is transparent, so we get the brilliance of "transmitted light" reflected off the white substrate, through the ink, and into the reader's eye. Colors are much truer and more luminous than those of opaque ink, from which light is reflected. Rotogravure reproduces sharp images on paper as coarse as newsprint, and so we get the brilliant color work of, say, the *New York Times Magazine,* on relatively poor-quality paper.

The Rise of Gravure

The first photographic intaglio printing plate was made by J. Nicéphore Niepce as early as 1814. Indeed, this was the first plate made by photography for any printing process. William Henry Fox Talbot, the British pioneer in photography, invented the method of using dichromated gelatin to control etching of a plate and patented the process in 1858. Karl Klic (also spelled Klietch or Klitsch) is the person most closely identified with gravure; his method, invented in 1879, has remained unchanged in principle. The first recorded gravure printing on a web press was done by the *Southend Standard,* a small, provincial British paper, in 1910. Two years later the method was perfected to a point where the *Illustrated London News* could use it for metropolitan-newspaper volume.

As recently as the late 1930s, A. Dultgen combined gravure with conventional halftone techniques. At about the same time, improvements in process-color techniques and the introduction of new synthetic-plastic printing surfaces and scanning devices markedly expanded the areas for gravure exploitation. Lately, the rapid expansion and improvement of cold-type composition has served to further enhance the capabilities of this process.

Sheet-fed gravure produces reproductions of continuous-tone art with the highest fidelity of any printing process. So it is not surprising that fine—and expensive—books of art masterpieces are printed by this intaglio method. American paper money is printed by intaglio as well; the plates are cut by hand with no photography involved. Moreover, for more than a century, all United States postage stamps were printed by intaglio; even today, while the use of lithography increases, intaglio still produces most of them.

Engraved stationery and other social printing, such as wedding invitations, announcements, calling cards, and the like, as well as commercial letterheads, envelopes, and business cards can be printed by intaglio. Such printing, which exudes an aura of elegance and richness, can be recognized by the raised image, which can always be felt and sometimes even seen. This is created by the embossing of the paper as it is pressed into the incised plate. A lower-cost method, thermography, also creates a raised image but is immediately recognized by the absence of the embossing or, more noticeably, of debossing on the reverse of the paper (for information on thermography, see chapter 17).

Tracing a Gravure Job

The vast percentage of gravure printing is, however, devoted to publications and advertising matter produced by web-fed presses. Tracing a typical job explains many facets of the process.

It all starts with a mechanical—a paste-up—which is converted to a transparent film. Type is typically cold type, photo or digitized. Line art is conventional, but continuous-tone originals are used instead of Veloxes or PMTs. For much work, especially periodicals such as locally edited Sunday magazines of newspapers, paste-ups are same-size. Other work, usually with less pressing deadlines, is done at a ratio of 1:1½ or even 1:2. The obvious reason is to minimize any defects by reducing them along with all other elements. Unlike the page negative of offset, gravure's final transparency must be a positive. So for a time, negative type images—white characters on a black background—were used for paste-up, while photographs (or other continuous-tone artwork) were transformed into negative images. But the processes involved were cumbersome and resulted in serious loss of details, so today it is customary to work with positive paste-ups and produce the final positive transparency photographically. And incidentally, there is no basic difference between paste-ups for gravure and those used for offset or letterpress.

A key element in rotogravure is the "carbon tissue," peculiarly named since neither carbon nor tissue is involved. A sheet of paper (whose only function is to be the bearer) is covered by that same dichromated gelatin that Fox Talbot used more than a century ago. While any alkaline chromate can be used, potassium dichromate is not only the least expensive but also comes closest to the ideal. When this gelatin is exposed to light through a transparency, it hardens in proportion to the intensity of that light when "developed" with plain hot water.

The carbon tissue is first exposed to a negative of a screen. While this is identical to the halftone screen used by other platemakers, it does not create the conventional halftone dot pattern. Instead, it defines the size of the myriad ink wells that will soon pock the copper cylinder. Now the positive transparency is exposed to the plate. Wherever light hits, the gelatin will harden. Because the grid of the screen has permitted maximum exposure to light, these intersecting lines are of greatest hardness in the gelatin. Type matter also produces maximum hardness. The various areas of a photograph harden the gelatin in precise relationship to the degree of light that has passed through the film.

The standard screen is 150 lines, much finer than that usually used for offset or letterpress. The halftone dot pattern is invisible to the naked eye at the fineness of 140 lines, so the rotogravure image is continuous tone as far as the reader can discern. But gravure screens even as fine as 300 lines are not really all that rare.

The carbon tissue, quite moist, is squeegeed onto the copper cylinder, where it affixes itself tightly. The image is now face down, the equivalent of flopping the negative in making a relief plate, which is necessary to create a mirror image on the plate so that the printed image is right-reading. Now the actual incising of the plate begins.

Perchloride of iron, a rather mild oxidant, is the etching agent or mordant. It works so slowly that 20 minutes to a half hour are needed to etch the plate. First, it must eat its way through the gelatin. Where the light has hardened the gelatin to the maximum (such as on the negative lines of the grid) the mordant never does work its way through to the metal. Where the positive image on the transparency (in the type characters, for instance) has barred all light, the gelatin is so soft that it does not delay the mordant at all; the perchloride eats at the plate for the entire period. Where an intermediate gray has allowed, let's say, passage of 50 percent of all potential light, the gelatin has hardened partially. The mordant needs about half the etching time to get through the carbon tissue, leaving only the other half of the time for etching the metal. The result, then, is a series of tiny wells defined by the screen—at least 22,500 per square inch—of varying depths.

The deeper the well, the more ink it holds and then deposits on the paper. The density of tone of the image depends on the depth of the ink. This is the same factor that affects the varying tones of a photograph. (It is the depth of silver oxide that varies the tones of a photograph.) Thus, rotogravure comes very close to being a continuous-tone image itself.

The etching platemaking process demands high skill from the platemaker, who will "stage out" various portions of the plate to reduce the time it is exposed to the mordant. Because type, for instance, requires only about half the etching time that pictures do, type areas are staged out—covered by a mordant-resistant varnish—during the first part of the process and are exposed to the mordant only in the final stages. Other areas may be isolated to receive more action from the etchant. Typically, a cylinder will be etched in four to six separate "bites," with action of the mordant being halted between bites by washing off the cylinder with plain water.

Cylinders can now be engraved electronically, a method that enjoys great favor with publications printers. A recent survey of the Gravure Technical Association reported that 76 percent of all cylinders used for such periodical work were etched electronically. For other kinds of work, though, chemical etching accounted for 93 percent of all cylinders. There are also mechanical methods of engraving, but they produce only a minuscule fraction of the 71,000 cylinders etched annually nationwide.

Resists other than carbon tissue are used for etching plates. Spray-ons are most popular, photopolymers are used less frequently, and silver-sensitive compounds quite rarely. The basic principles remain unchanged, though.

The time of exposure of the transparency to the carbon tissue will vary quite extensively, depending on the tonal variations of the images involved. Proper exposure times are more accurately determined by skilled human eyes than by any electronic or optical measuring devices. Even before this exposure, human judgment must choose which carbon tissue to use, as there are several different kinds, each designed for specific types of reproduction and/or for varying conditions of heat and humidity during the process.

The transfer of the gelatin from the paper bearer to the cylinder also demands great skill. One of the dangers during this stage is that the dimensions of the gelatin may be distorted. Because the tissue must be wetted at several stages of its manufacture, the usual swelling and shrinking occurs as paper fibers absorb and then lose moisture. The gelatin itself is about as firm as a dish of Jell-O and has little dimensional stability.

The various bites in the actual etching process are usually the result of different concentrations of the mordant; the craftsperson must determine, often by instinct, which strength is desired at any of the various stages. The platemaker, sometimes using instruments but more often just a trained eye, must determine when the etching processes have gone to their desired ends. And it is possible to correct defects in the finished cylinder by delicate and painstaking manual procedures. All these processes emphasize the need for skilled technicians.

The platemaker must work within extremely narrow tolerances. For comparatively "rough" work, such as packages and labels, a maximum depth of .002 inch is used; superior color work requires ink wells of only half that depth. Postage stamps and similar fine work will have incisions as shallow as .0007 inch.

The proofing or checking of gravure work is of comparatively recent vintage. It was not until after World War II that proof presses for rotogravure were available. Before that time, visual errors were spotted and corrected on the paste-up, and mechanical deficiencies were noted and corrected, if possible, on the cylinder itself.

Reverse Halftone Process

A variation of conventional rotogravure is the reverse halftone process. While there are several versions—the Henderson and the Huebner processes are popular—the best known is the Dultgen (named after its inventor) or Dultgen-News process. In the letterpress halftone plate, dots of varying shape and size are raised from the bearing surface of the plate. The ratio of ink areas deposited by such dots to surrounding white paper creates the illusion of varying values of gray. In reverse halftones, the halftone dots, instead of being raised, are depressed below the bearing surface. The illusion of gray is still obtained by the optical mixing of the differing areas of ink deposited by these wells on the background paper. This effect, though, is heightened not only by varying that area of the dots but also by varying the amount of ink in each dot, depending on the depth of the incised wells.

An advantage to this method is the longer life of the plate, because all the wells are relatively deeper and therefore can withstand more abrasion before the image is distorted. Moreover, etching can be more easily controlled, and it is also simpler to make exact duplicate plates from one set of positives. Corrections of tone—and especially color—can be made more readily, because it is easier to control the area of a well than it is its depth.

Fidelity to the original art is not as precise in reverse halftones as it is with conventional gravure. There is a tendency for light areas to print darker than desired. Images tend to be a bit fuzzy, and sometimes the dot pattern is too obvious. Yet reverse halftones remain popular with newspapers.

Another interesting variation on the basic method is a combination of gravure and offset. The printed image is transferred from the intaglio cylinder to a rubber blanket and from there set off onto the printing paper. All the advantages of offset obtain, primarily that the resilience of the rubber blanket permits fine images to be printed on papers that are too hard or too rough for direct printing.

The Many Uses of Gravure

The strengths and advantages of gravure are perhaps best demonstrated by its users; someone needing printing might well consider this when deciding which method to use. Of the billions of dollars generated by the gravure industry each year, publication printing is responsible for almost a half. The three largest-circulation magazines in the United States—*Parade, TV Guide,* and *National Enquirer*—are printed by rotogravure, as are 18 of the 25 top-circulation magazines. Sunday magazines in American newspapers have been major users of gravure since its introduction.

Newspaper inserts are another giant consumer of gravure. These range from single sheets to full tabloid sections. They become a part of the newspaper but are not classed as regular supplements, such as the Sunday magazines or special editions produced by local advertising staffs.

These inserts have virtually replaced an interesting category, also printed by gravure, called preprints. These are ads (and, rarely, editorial pictures) printed by gravure on rolls of paper, as is the newspaper itself. But, after printing, instead of being cut and folded into the familiar newspaper "book," the web is rerolled. This roll is sent to the newspaper involved, where, in the regular press run, material such as the name and address of local merchants is printed on the ad; the back of the sheet is printed with current news and ad material.

Advertising is almost profligate in its use of intaglio. Direct-mail advertisers, whose mailings frequently exceed the million mark, find rotogravure an ideal process. Typical are the promotional campaigns of book and record clubs. With mailings nearing 2 million and full-color reproductions of book jackets and record covers used profusely, the industries can maintain brilliant color while using only common newsprint. (For more on direct-mail printing, see chapter 15.)

A fast-growing advertising medium in America is catalogs, and gravure has staked a substantial claim in this area. (By definition, catalogs are booklets of 16 or more bound pages.) Of all mass-merchandising catalogs, gravure produced 90 percent. The top mail-order sellers all use gravure-printed catalogs: J.C. Penney, Sears, and Spiegel.

Advertising matter such as direct-mail, other display advertising and newspaper inserts that are distributed door-to-door or in-store rather than with the newspaper, and commercial printing—including such interesting items as Christmas and playing cards and gridded chart paper, not to mention annual reports and financial and bank printing other than currency—accounted for $3.5 billion worth of production in 1981. The printing of stamps and paper money, already noted, runs to billions of impressions annually in this country alone, and the volume increases constantly.

Another growing field served by gravure is the printing and converting of packaging. The beginning of self-service groceries in the 1930s and the extension of that retailing technique to other stores, notably drugstores, required the prepackaging of merchandise that previously had been sold in bulk and packaged at the moment of purchase. Self-service required prepackaged merchandise for shelf display and check-out convenience. Frozen foods, which came soon after, obviously had to be packaged, not only for selling but for the actual quick-freezing process. Soon the most common foods, such as navy beans and frankfurters, which had been sold in bulk for generations, began to be packaged.

Besides faster service, prepackaging also provides potent point-of-purchase advertising. So as the packaging industry grows in all kinds of economic cycles, rotogravure's share of packaging also grows apace. A contributing factor has been the invention and improvement of machines that wrap merchandise at the rate of well over 200 per minute. Such machines require wrappers in roll form, and it is simple for rotogravure to print from a web and reroll wrappers just as it rerolls preprinted newspaper ads.

A constant stream of new and improved wrapping materials also increases gravure's market. Such plastics as cellophane, the various acetates, Pliofilm and Saran, and aluminum foil need special kinds of ink that rotogravure can handle easily. Fast-drying inks are required; these synthetic wrappings will not absorb ink. The ink must adhere to a hard and slippery surface and must resist rub-off. Appropriate inks use resins and binders such as nitrocellulose, which literally bites into the hard plastic surface of the wrappers.

Aluminum foil poses an interesting problem to the best printers and printing methods. Practical as packaging, striking as display, the foil makes a desirable substrate even as it challenges the printer. Mounted directly on a color press, a machine laminates foil to paper, film, or board, and prints it all in one operation. Butter, margarine, and soap wrappers are everyday examples of this major and growing field for rotogravure.

Labels are another important part of the packaging trade, accounting for half a billion dollars in annual volume. And the newest kind of packaging attests to the versatility of gravure. This is the so-called retortable pouch, an envelope of plastic that can be dropped into boiling water to heat the food it contains. It serves as another reminder that ever since Gutenberg, the graphic arts have grown and expanded with almost every new development in any other field of industry or human interest.

We do not usually associate printing processes with floor coverings, but that category accounts for hundreds of millions of dollars in annual gravure production. Huge cylinders, some as wide as 16 feet, print and emboss patterns in one operation. In 1981 alone, three trillion—yes, trillion—82 billion square feet of cushioned vinyl flooring was produced in both sheet and tile form, and every bit of it was done by gravure. Other vinyl products, such as wall coverings, auto and furniture upholstery, auto interiors, shower curtains, lawn umbrellas—the list is long and eclectic—are mostly made by gravure. Perhaps best known are the coverings for walls and counters in patterns and wood grains. Humans improve upon nature by manufacturing laminated materials such as wallboard, which is not only stronger than natural wood but whose printed grain is far more pronounced than that of true timber.

Wallpaper was long printed by hand-engraved cylinders, so the switch to rotogravure printing was easy and logical.

At least 70 percent of the homely paper towels and toilet tissues that we take for granted have color patterns and often embossing done by gravure. Rotogravure techniques are employed in making steel cylinders that are used for die-stamping in paper and other materials.

Planning a Gravure Job

Although such a wide range of uses makes any accurate summary quite difficult, the slogan of the industry is to the point: if you want high quality in long runs at economical prices, choose gravure.

As the cost of making a gravure cylinder is relatively high, the method requires press-runs long enough to make the per-copy preparatory cost feasible. A rule of thumb says that the method becomes cost-effective at a minimum run of just below the 100,000 mark. There is no practical upper limit.

Rotogravure should be considered when high fidelity of continuous-tone art is required, especially in color. This is why sheet-fed gravure is used for the finest books of art reproductions. But the advantage exists even on the other end of the economic printing scale, with fine color work on relatively cheap newsprint.

There is no line work in gravure, so a job that has much line matter is not well suited to this process. Photographs make ideal gravure copy. With the fine screens available and the modulation of ink thickness already noted, gravure can make reproductions of photographs that even a practiced eye can often not tell from the original. Watercolors, pencil, pastels, and charcoal are excellent media for gravure reproduction. So are oil paintings, if a smooth surface is maintained. Impasto techniques, which pile paint into obvious three-dimensional areas, are less desirable, since the brush or palette-knife strokes are exaggerated unpleasantly by gravure.

Whatever the medium, it needs well-defined middle tones for gravure reproduction. Photographs should not have too much contrast; on the other hand, soft-focus photos will be further softened by gravure, and this effect must be remembered when shots are selected for a job.

Type matter is, of course, line work. Obviously, it is ridiculous to think of any commercial printing without type, so here the admonition against line gravure must be tempered by common sense. All type will be softened (some might say made mushy) by the gravure screen. This is because the sharpest of lines on the original art are constantly being interrupted by the grid of the intaglio wells. While this serration is far beyond visibility by the naked eye, even in images much larger than body type, the overall effect is present in any-size type and should be mitigated.

It is best to use no body type smaller than 10-point for gravure. Modern roman types, with their thin hairlines and serifs, are particularly susceptible to the breaking of those fine lines. So it is wise, as a matter of principle, to choose old-style romans, sans serifs, or square serifs for body type.

The effective life of a gravure cylinder—an important economic factor—depends on many things. The greatest wear comes from the scraping action of the doctor blade. Normally, the ink acts as a lubricant, and wear is minimized. On the other hand, dried particles of ink, dust, and other foreign matter that may get into the ink fountain will either act as abrasives or will require greater pressure by the doctor blade, and thus greater cylinder wear, to achieve a clean wipe. The comparatively coarse surface of newsprint will wear down the copper much more quickly than will the smoother surface of book paper. Typically, when printing on the paper usually used for periodicals on a web press, with ink ducts open to possible contamination, a cylinder will produce from 60,000 to 100,000 good impressions. If the ink supply is protected from foreign matter, the run can go as high as 500,000 impressions. Plates on sheet-fed presses are generally of shorter life, about 50,000 impressions.

In all instances, printing life can be extended by facing the cylinder with a thin layer—.001 inch—of chromium. This can reasonably assure a quality of image up to a million, and longer runs are not unusual.

Safety Hazards

One disadvantage to any rotogravure process is the fire and explosion hazard. (This is, of course, of no immediate concern to the buyer of printing.) All gravure inks, except water-based ones, give off vapors that are highly flammable and even explosive. Smoking is strictly forbidden in gravure pressrooms, and any source of static electricity that might produce a lethal spark is tightly controlled if not eliminated. In many instances craftspeople are not allowed to wear rubber-soled shoes, lest static build up in their bodies. Antistatic devices include the old-fashioned but effective hanging of Christmas-tree tinsel on the press. By using enclosed ink fountains, vapors that might endanger health as well as cause fire dangers are trapped and, in effect, recycled in the ink.

Technology in Gravure

As in all the graphic-arts processes, electronic scanners are playing an increasingly large role in gravure platemaking. This is especially notable in the electronic engraving of plates already noted and in digitized color separation. Electronic color previewers allow the printer to simulate the appearance of the final printed image from the original color transparency, and color corrections can begin even before making the actual color separation.

At the moment, this device is used only for periodical printing. It is inevitable, though, that it will soon expand into all fields of gravure platemaking. One benefit will be a reduction in the use of photographic film. Fluctuations in the silver market have driven such materials to costs that disturb the industry, especially since gravure requires more film—both negative and positive—than do other printing processes. Electronic engraving will lower film consumption and costs significantly.

Gravure Presses

Standard cylinder circumferences range from 21 to 111 inches, and the same numbers describe standard widths, although we have already noted the 192-inch widths used for floor covering. Copper sheets used for gravure run from 16 by 19½ inches to 30½ by 40 inches. These are listed as "99.99 percent pure copper." The purer the metal, the more cleanly and truly it will etch. These sheets are used as flat plates or—because they are only .03 inch thick—are wrapped around cylinders.

Web width on gravure presses ranges from 24 inches to 156 inches, with a median of 75 inches. In addition to these "standard" dimensions, which apply to conventional printing, there are many specialized presses. The rotogravure user should canvass the market before deciding on a purveyor.

Conclusion

In the traditional three-way contest among letterpress, lithography, and gravure as dollar producers, gravure is still third, but it is consistently taking a larger share of the market. By 1981, gravure produced 16 percent of all printing dollars, compared with 19 percent for letterpress and 45 percent for offset. Flexography accounted for 15 percent and miscellaneous methods the other 5 percent. Analysts predict substantial growth for gravure during the next five-year period.

Gravure is closely linked to industries that are in a rapid growth pattern: publications, advertising inserts, packaging, and catalogs. Gravure expects to increase its publications volume 20 percent in the next five years, inserts 18 percent, packaging 14.8 percent, and catalogs 21 percent. Improvements in supporting graphic arts areas—scanners, nonsilver photography, electronic engravers, and major refinements in bindery operations—seem a bit tilted toward gravure's advantage.

The ancient armorer who first recorded his incised patterns would certainly be amazed if he could see how far his simple printing process has expanded.

How to Use 6
Screen Printing

Screen printing, the modern term for the silk-screen process, is the youngest, most versatile, and possibly the most rapidly developing of the major graphic arts systems. Many people, including those involved in other branches of the printing industry, still tend to think of screen printing as a relatively crude method. Indeed, the progress in screen printing is not widely known outside its own industry. People who have "seen screen printing being done" may find the real state of progress difficult to believe, especially if their only contact has been to visit one of the small shops where simple, manual printing methods are still used.

Many such small shops produce good work and form a substantial part of the industry. The basic principles of screen printing are so simple that for short-run production and special market requirements, manual printing is still profitable. Modern screen inks and photo-stencil systems are all available to the small shop, and industry sources can supply services such as camera work and screen making if these are beyond the capacity of the shop.

Because of these wide differences in production methods—between the small shop and the large, highly mechanized plant—a first impression of screen printing can be very inadequate, if not confusing. Therefore, the important functions of this chapter will be to (1) clearly define what screen printing is, (2) review its present stage of development, and (3) offer a guide to the advantages of screen printing in certain fields of application.

Such a guide is of value to the print user, advertising agency, or manufacturer, as there are special features of screen printing that make it more suitable than any other printing system for certain types of printing work. Although the older and better-known characteristics of screen printing—such as its ability to print solid areas of bright, opaque colors—may be desirable under certain circumstances, new applications have been achieved through technological developments that may broaden screen printing's appeal.

Principles of Screen Printing

Essentially, screen printing is a stencil process. Historical writers have linked it with early decorative or religious stenciled-image crafts. But the distinguishing feature of screen printing is the use of a stretched mesh fabric, or "screen," which acts as both the supporting structure for the stencil and a carrier for the ink during the printing action.

It is the important function of holding the stencil that enables a continuous image to be printed around an island form, like the center of the letter o, which in the conventional stencil has to be held by ties or bridges left in the cutting of the stencil. The screen system also enables fine and intricate detail to be printed. In the case of half-tones, a fine mesh holds the very small stencil discs that form the reverse dots in the shadow areas.

The second function of the screen—acting as a carrier for the ink—is an essential part of the printing action. In its usual form of operation (there are variations), screen printing is done with a squeegee. This is a straight-edged rubber or plastic blade, inclined at an angle and drawn across the surface of the screen, with a supply of ink in front of the blade edge. The moving squeegee drives ink through the mesh in the open areas of the stencil, causing an image to be printed on the material or substrate under the screen.

Repetition of the action—replacing the printed copy each time with the next sheet in the run and replenishing ink on the screen when necessary—enables continuous printing to be maintained throughout the length of the run.

In manual screen printing, the squeegee is a hand-held implement, usually made of wood, with the blade secured in a groove. In mechanized screen printing, the squeegee is of special design, and its movements are automatically controlled. It can be preset for angle, pressure, and sweep speed. These variables, which have a considerable influence on print quality, will remain constant.

Most forms of mechanized screen printing have developed from the original, manual printing unit, illustrated in figure 6–1. In its basic form, this is a frame on which the screen fabric is stretched and then hinged at one end to a flat board that serves as a printing base. A "swing leg" or prop keeps the frame up so that paper or other material may be laid on the base. Together with the squeegee for printing, this comprises a complete production unit. Figure 6–2 shows the essential elements involved in producing a screen-printed image.

The effect by which a printed image is produced on the substrate is widely believed, even by screen printers themselves, to be the result of "pressing" the ink through the screen, with squeegee pressure as the main factor. In reality, the action is a lot more complicated, involving fluid pressure produced by a hydrodynamic effect. This results when the semifluid ink is moved across the screen by the angled squeegee blade, as shown in figure 6–3. To obtain the highest-quality printing, the variables in the action must be correctly balanced.

A suitable mesh fabric for early screen printing was readily available in the form of pure silk gauzes used by grain millers as sifting meshes for refining flour. This strong, resilient fabric was ideal for the new printing method, which became known as the silk-screen process.

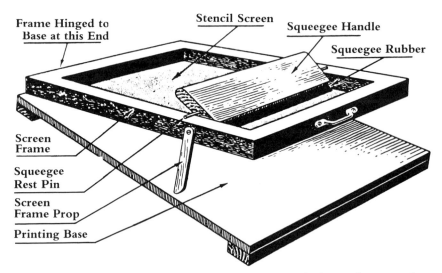

Figure 6-1. A hand-operated screen-printing unit, on which any flat material can be printed. Many screen-printing presses are based on this mechanism.

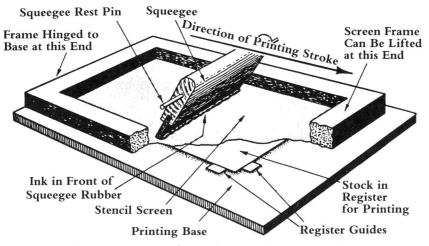

Squeegee Rest Pin   Squeegee

Frame Hinged to
Base at this End

Direction of Printing Stroke

Screen Frame
Can Be Lifted
at this End

Ink in Front of
Squeegee Rubber

Stencil Screen

Printing Base

Stock in
Register
for Printing

Register Guides

Figure 6-2. View of a simple set-up for screen printing.

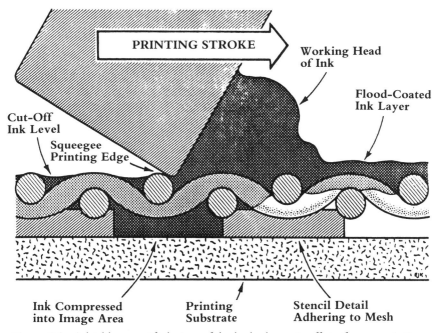

PRINTING STROKE

Working Head
of Ink

Flood-Coated
Ink Layer

Cut-Off
Ink Level

Squeegee
Printing Edge

Ink Compressed
into Image Area

Printing
Substrate

Stencil Detail
Adhering to Mesh

Figure 6-3. A highly magnified view of the hydrodynamic effect of screen printing. The angled squeegee creates fluid pressure, which drives the ink through the open areas of the stencil.

Although some silk screens are still used, most modern screens are composed of synthetic mesh materials such as nylon and polyester. Screens made of fine, stainless-steel wire cloth are used in jobs for which great durability is required, such as industrial screen printing. All these materials can be obtained in much finer weaves than silk, and being monofilament (single cylindrical thread) structures (see figure 6–4), they are more suitable for printing purposes than are multifilament silk fabrics.

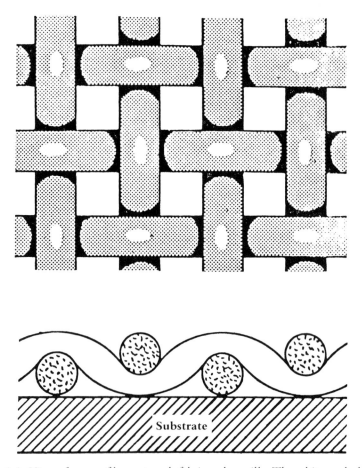

Figure 6-4. View of a monofilament mesh fabric such as silk. The white ovals depict small "knuckle" areas of the mesh that actually come into contact with the substrate.

Advantages and Applications of Screen Printing

A primary advantage of early screen printing was the low cost of the simple, manually operated equipment. Preparation costs were also much lower than those of other printing systems. Hand-cut stencils, for example, were much cheaper than wooden letterpress blocks or metal lithographic plates (see chapter 3 on lithography and chapter 4 on letterpress).

Sign painters were among the first to use screen printing and found it to have many practical advantages. In addition to using it for paper posters and signs, one could screen-print banners on calico, pennants on felt, signs on wood or metal, or various other work on glass, leather, or textiles. There seemed no limit to the applications for this versatile process. It was also without rival for printing bright, solid colors. What other process could print white on black in a single pass?

Although modern screen printing has been developed and expanded to suit a whole range of markets and new technologies, many graphics and manufacturing industries today are still well served by the more traditional screen-printing processes.

Advertising, display, and point-of-purchase: Posters, signs, and other promotional materials can be screen printed on paper or paperboard. Screen-printed window displays, cutouts, cards, and tickets are effective, and high-impact advertising matter can be screen printed in fluorescent colors. Supermarket shelf displays and self-service selling aids can also come under this category.

Metal signs and outdoor advertising: Screen printing is used to produce permanent advertising signs and billboards, highway warning and direction signs, and other items that require long-term resistance to weather and the elements.

Textiles and wallpaper printing: These two are grouped together, since similar machinery is used to produce them both. For example, the same manufacturer may turn out printed furnishing fabrics, curtains, and wallcoverings. An allied industry produces screen-printed dress fabrics.

Garment imprinting: Technically a form of textile printing, the imprinting of sportswear and T-shirts is an entirely separate—and growing—industry. Specially designed screen-printing machinery can imprint graphics directly onto garments. The industry also produces heat-applied transfers for decorating garments, although not all of these are screen printed. Some are produced by offset lithography.

Transfers and self-adhesive labels: Originally used to print water-based decal transfers, this technique is now largely used to print on pressure-sensitive, self-adhesive materials. For example, screen-printed ceramic decals are used for decorating kiln-fired glassware and pottery.

Packaging: This is a large industry using special machinery for screen printing directly on bottles, jars, and other packaging containers made of glass or plastic. Machinery designs and imprinting techniques are so well developed that objects or containers of almost any shape can be screen printed (see figure 6–5).

Other industrial applications: Many screen applications occur in-plant as part of a manufacturer's production of larger items. These include screen-printed toys and games; dials and scales printed for clocks, watches, automobile instruments, and radio-tuning; and operational markings on appliances such as gas or electric stoves, refrigerators, and washing machines.

Electronics and circuit printing: This is a large and expanding field for nongraphic applications. It includes the printing of etching resists for copper-clad laminate circuit boards, the printing of actual conducting circuits on ceramic wafers, and larger work such as screen-printed heating elements on automobile rear windows. It also covers the printing of etching resists for the so-called chemical machining method of manufacturing small metal parts.

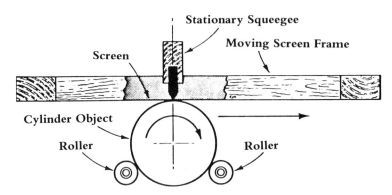

Figure 6-5. View of how a cylindrical object, such as a bottle, is screen printed. The moving screen turns the object under the stationary squeegee.

History of Screen Printing

New applications for screen printing are continually being found, often to answer the needs of developing technologies in other industries. It has been said that astronauts could not have landed on the Moon, nor could satellites orbit the Earth, were it not for the miniaturized circuitry made possible by screen printing.

Screen printing in this country began around 1910, and the British Patent No. 756—the earliest known screen-printing patent—was filed by Samuel Simon of Manchester, England, in 1907. Compared with the invention of movable type for letterpress by Johann Gutenberg more than 500 years ago and the discovery of lithography by Alois Senefelder more than 180 years ago, one can appreciate the rapid development of screen printing. It is now regarded by printing technologists as the fourth major system, the other three being letterpress, offset lithography, and gravure.

In heading a new group in its own right—stencil printing—screen printing has the distinction of being the only system in which ink passes right through the printing plate. Some of the system's characteristics will be discussed after noting how power presses have replaced the manual printing action.

Screen-Printing Presses

Most screen-printing machines for general production are flatbeds. The work is laid to register on a flatbed or printing base, and printed by a power-driven squeegee, as shown in figure 6–6. The terms *semi-automatic* and *fully automatic* refer to the degree of automatic action applied to the "feed, print, and remove" cycle.

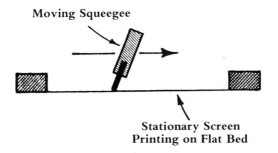

Moving Squeegee

Stationary Screen Printing on Flat Bed

Figure 6-6. The basic action of flatbed screen printing (the bed itself is not shown).

The first term usually denotes hand feeding and removal of the work, with a powered printing action combined with an automatic rise-and-fall movement of the screen frame (see figure 6–7). Fully automatic production involves complete mechanization of sheet feeding, printing, delivery to a conveyorized dryer, and automatic sheet piling at the delivery end (see figure 6–8). It is "press-button" screen printing, using separate, functional units coupled together to form a complete production line.

Screen press manufacturers often build their own dryers, but sheet-

Figure 6-7. A semiautomatic screen printing press. (Courtesy of American Screen Printing Equipment Co., an Advance Group company)

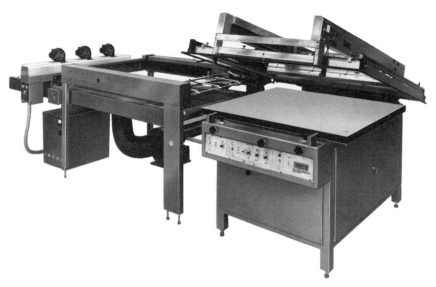

Figure 6-8. A fully automatic screen-printing press, fitted with sheet take-off and UV curing module. (Courtesy of American Screen Printing Equipment Co., an Advance Group company)

feeder units are so well developed for other printing systems that standard types are usually coupled to screen presses. Most large screen-printing plants have one or more fully automatic lines.

Cylinder presses work on a different principle, using a rotating impression cylinder instead of a flat printing bed, as shown in figure 6–9. The leading edge of the sheet is fed to grippers on the cylinder, and the screen frame moves horizontally to match the surface speed of the cylinder. In this action, the squeegee is stationary and produces line-contact printing on the curved surface of the sheet, which is fed through and delivered to the dryer. The squeegee then rises slightly, and the screen frame returns to its starting position for the next impression.

Cylinder presses (see figure 6–10) are generally faster than flatbeds; on smaller sheet sizes their speed can be in the range of 5,000 impressions per hour. (In comparison, flatbeds can handle from 1,200 to 3,000 impressions per hour.) The cylinder press is primarily a machine for fully automatic operation on long runs.

All modern screen presses, including manual equipment, make use

**Moving Screen Frame
Printing on Cylinder**

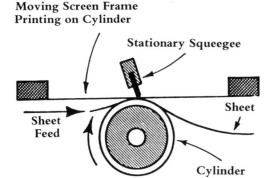

*Figure 6-9. The basic action
of a cylinder screen printing
press, which prints on a
rotating impression cylinder.*

of both vacuum action to hold the work on the bed or cylinder and
what is called the "off-contact" printing technique. This means that
the screen is set a short distance above the printing surface, with
which it is brought into a momentary line-contact under the squeegee
edge. The resilience and tension of the mesh is a factor in this action,
which improves detail and sharpness of halftone dots.

Rotary Screen Printing

The rotary system is the screen-printing equivalent of the rotary or
web press used in other forms of printing (see figure 6–11). Instead
of a flat printing screen, it uses rotating cylindrical screens with in-

*Figure 6-10. A cylinder screen printing press, fitted with sheet feeder and UV curing
units. (Courtesy of General Research, Inc.)*

Figure 6-11. A multicolor rotary or web press for screen printing, used for high-speed production of tags, labels, and decals. (Courtesy of General Research, Inc.)

ternal ink supply and squeegee action. The screens are usually made of thin stainless steel, with finely spaced perforations for the ink to come through.

Rotary screen printing is most suited to the continuous decoration of material by a web system. The work passes between the printing cylinder and an impression cylinder, which rotates under the web, as shown in figure 6–12. It is used, for example, to produce textiles and wallpapers on presses that can print up to 20 different colors.

The enclosed squeegee action prevents manual replenishment of

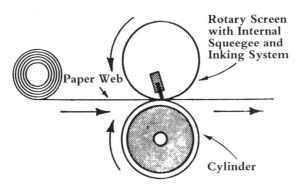

Figure 6-12. The basic action of a rotary or web screen printing press. A cylindrical screen is used with an internal squeegee and inking system.

ink while the press is running. Therefore, rotary screen-printing machines have automatic ink-feeding systems combined with the squeegee action so that fast, continuous operation can be maintained. The rotary system also uses several unusual types of squeegees. One features a flexible metal blade, another has a roller action, and yet another is magnetic.

Stencil-making Methods

In principle, a stencil for screen printing is produced by masking or blocking out the nonimage areas on the screen mesh. There are numerous ways of doing this. One of the earliest was the blockout method (described in Samuel Simon's 1907 patent), in which the nonimage areas are painted out on the screen mesh with a filler or blockout solution. Hand-cut stencils can be made with paper or specially prepared commercial cutting films, which are laminated onto a transparent backing sheet. Such stencils are made by a cut-and-peel procedure, in which the backing sheet is removed after the stencil has been adhered to the screen with a solvent.

Starting in the 1930s, the manufacture of solvent-adhering stencil film was an important influence in beginning a new era of better quality in the growing screen-printing industry. The cut-and-peel idea, with fine detail and island forms held on the backing sheet until transferred to the mesh, enabled the stencil cutter to develop new degrees of skill. The hand-cut stencil was bridging the gap between earlier, crude stencil methods and the increasing use of photographic systems.

Photographic Stencils

At a relatively early period, photographic stencils, based on the dichromated colloid action used in other graphic arts processes, were developed for the use of the screen printer. Essentially, these systems involve a colloid substance, such as glue or gelatin, sensitized with potassium or ammonium dichromate. Exposure to actinic light through a positive transparency makes the nonimage areas insoluble, thus allowing the image areas to be dissolved and washed out.

Stencils for screen printing are exposed through a hand-drawn or photographic positive transparency, held in close contact with the light-sensitive preparation. On completion of the procedures, the image areas of the printing screen are open for the passage of ink. The advent of photo-stencils made possible the printing of very fine detail and halftones, which the early silk-screen process was incapable of achieving.

Modern photo-stencil systems are divided into three distinct groups, as illustrated in figure 6–13:

1. *Direct-emulsion coatings:* These comprise light-sensitive liquid emulsions for coating the screen, often by multiple applications. When

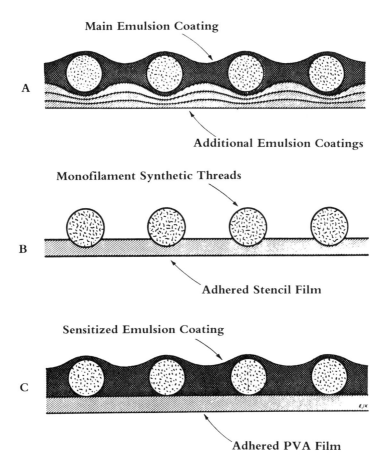

Figure 6-13. Magnified views of the three types of photostencil systems: (a) direct-emulsion coatings; (b) indirect film stencils; and (c) direct-indirect method.

dry, the sensitized screen is exposed in direct contact with a positive transparency of the required image. The soluble image areas are then sprayed clear with water.

2. *Indirect film stencils:* Indirect stencils are exposed and developed before being adhered to the screen mesh. Most of today's indirect materials are presensitized films ready-coated on a clear support, and exposure is through the positive transparency in contact with the support. The procedures are very simple and quick.

3. *Direct-indirect methods:* With these systems (also called film-emulsion), a thin film of polyvinyl acetate is adhered to the underside of the screen fabric by a sensitized emulsion squeegeed through the screen from above. The film itself takes up sensitizer from the emulsion before the coating dries. Exposure and washout are the same as for direct-emulsion coatings.

These three groups of photo-stencil systems have somewhat different characteristics. Direct-emulsion coatings encapsulate the mesh threads and bond very firmly to the screen fabric, producing tough stencils capable of very long press-runs, up to 200,000 or more impressions. Indirect films bond only by surface adhesion with light bedding into the mesh. Although these stencils are excellent for printing very fine detail and halftones, they are relatively weak compared with direct emulsions. Direct-indirect stencils belong to a hybrid group offering the durability of the direct-emulsion coating with the fine detail qualities of the indirect method.

During recent years, changes in relative cost factors have caused a wide swing to direct-emulsion stencils. The large production and marketing investments at stake in indirect stencil systems, however, seem to be reflected in the more recent development of new types of these films designed to regain the indirect stencil's share of the market. Improved adhesion, longer run life, and rapid nonchemical processing are offered in one type of film. Also, a new form of direct-indirect product has been developed, in which a presensitized film is adhered with water in place of a sensitized emulsion.

Screen Mesh Fabrics

Although there is still some demand for silk fabrics, the screen-printing industry in general has switched to the monofilament nylon and polyester fabrics previously mentioned. These synthetic materials have proved to be far superior to silk in meeting the demands of modern, high-quality screen printing. There are several reasons for this. Monofilament mesh structures, including wire cloth, allow ink to pass more freely through the fabric than is possible with the fibrous thread structure of silk. Synthetics are also available in much finer weaves than silk—up to 508 threads per inch, as compared with 200 threads per inch for the finest silk.

As a general rule, fine meshes are needed for fine detail, as the weave structure influences the image edge and definition. Fine-mesh fabrics also use less ink. The thickness of the wet ink film is determined by the amount of ink held in the mesh at the instant of printing, this being the amount remaining on the substrate when the screen lifts. Mesh fineness is also a very important factor in avoiding the so-called moiré effect in halftone printing. In conventional printing systems, the moiré effect (a visually distracting, rippled pattern) often occurs when a halftone is rescreened from an existing halftone and the two sets of halftone dots overlap and clash.

Screen printing is prone to a built-in moiré problem of its own, as an interference effect can be caused by a clash between the halftone dots and the regularly spaced mesh threads. In practice, this is easily avoided by using a mesh not less than three times as fine as the halftone dot count.

Inks and Drying Systems

Because it is adaptable to printing on almost any type of natural or synthetic material, as well as on three-dimensional objects, screen printing uses more varieties of ink than does any other printing system. In addition to numerous inks for paper and paperboard applications, totally different inks serve specialized purposes, such as printing transfers and self-adhesives, textiles, ceramics, plastics, metal signs, and instrument dials and scales. There are also nongraphic screening preparations, including adhesives, etching resists, and special metallic conducting pastes for printing circuits and switching devices.

Most of these inks present special drying problems because of the nature of the system. Screen-printing deposits a heavier ink film than any other printing system, due to its action, in which a relatively large amount of ink is held in the mesh structure and transferred to the substrate when the screen lifts. In general, the finer the mesh, the thinner the ink film. Another factor is the thickness of the stencil between the mesh and the substrate, although this only applies near the stencil edge or across the width of narrow lines or dots; in larger areas the mesh dips into contact with the substrate.

Nearly all modern screen inks are of the solvent-based type, which dries by evaporation, and drying has always been a problem because of the large amount of solvent in the relatively heavy ink film. With screen printing one cannot, as with other printing systems, print and pile printed materials directly from the press; there has to be a drying phase, and with the development of power presses and higher printing speeds, the problem increases. The old method of racking prints by hand has long been inadequate. True mechanized drying started with the "wicket dryer," an endless moving system of wire wickets that receives prints from the press and exposes them to air long enough for them to dry before being dropped into a pile. These dryers are often as much as 60 feet long.

One very important point about the drying process: although the work should dry as rapidly as possible (ideally it should come dry from the press), the ink must not dry in the screen while the press is running, since it would then not make contact. Jet-air dryers have been developed to ensure faster drying and reduce the floor space required for the equipment. The work is fed onto a conveyor passing under jets of hot air, followed by a cooling stage to restore the dimensional state of the paper.

Various radiation drying systems, including infrared, have been adapted to screen printing. Within the last 10 years, ultraviolet (UV) drying (or more correctly "curing") has attracted a lot of attention, and the method has been progressively developed. The UV system employs specially formulated inks which, under UV radiation, are converted to a solid state by an almost instant polymerization (change in the molecular structure). One of the properties of the inks is that they do not evaporate, so there are no problems of fine detail drying in the mesh.

Conventional screen inks and drying systems are coming under pressures that can only increase in the long term. Solvent-based inks use large amounts of petroleum derivatives, which are affected by increasing costs and the eventual fate of oil as a nonrenewable energy source. But a more immediate pressure, already felt in most industrialized countries, comes from a general trend in rules imposed under industrial health and safety legislation.

Solvent vapors are known to be toxic in the workplace, and they add to environmental pollution if they are vented out of the workplace. The great interest in UV-cured screen ink systems is not only because they offer instant drying from press to pile but also because UV inks give off no vapors and are nonpolluting. Another solution may come from further development of water-based screen inks. Already widely used for printing textiles and T-shirts, water-based inks give off no toxic vapors, and only water is needed for screen and press washups.

How to Choose Screen Printing

Modern screen printing has firmly established itself since the old days of the silk-screen process, when it was regarded with tolerant amusement by the established graphic-reproduction industry. Not only is it capable of extremely good quality standards but its adaptability has given it fields of application where it has no rivals.

Printing systems, however, tend to be judged by their performance in the more widely known graphic fields, where the quality standards are recognized. How good is the system's definition in fine detail? Can it print small type? How fine a line can it print? How good is its halftone reproduction? And above all, for its commercial appeal, what is the quality of its four-color halftone reproduction? But before giving guidelines for what can be expected in quality, here is some basic advice for print buyers or clients new to this branch of the graphic arts.

Screen printing is a widely diversified industry. A printer may have a small shop in a garage or a fully mechanized plant employing many people. Some do general screen printing, while others work in specialized fields. But generally, if you want a certain type of work—and particularly if you want top quality—go to a specialist in that field.

Forget a lot of the things you thought you knew about screen printing. "Typical screen printing" dates back to when you could actually see the mesh marks and feel the heavy buildup of the ink with your fingertips. Never say, "That's not screen printed!" when shown work that looks and feels like good offset lithography. It may very well be screen printed and merely look like good offset. Even a microscope may reveal no characteristic difference.

Ask to see printed samples of the screen printer's work. Most screen printers in the high-quality area will be pleased to show it to you, and may have a display area for this purpose. But screen printers do tend to specialize, so if you want four-color halftone work in fine-screen (over 100-line), don't be surprised if you can't get it from a poster printer who specializes in coarse-screen work; your work won't fit into his production capabilities. Go to a specialist who produces fine four-color work for close-up viewing, such as in-store displays for jewelry or cosmetics. The kind of work you want can always be done if you go to the right place.

Another important point: in many cases, screen printing should not be regarded as a cheap alternative or competitor to the other established printing systems. Mechanized screen printing is economical for short-run jobs because of its simple preparation, while manual screen printing still holds its own for very short press-runs. Furthermore, faster presses and more efficient drying systems have combined to make screen printing competitive with short-run offset. On the other hand, screen printing is never likely to be competitive with offset for long press-runs. Not only are offset presses faster but the ink consumption—and cost—is lower.

Screen printing has qualities of its own. A good starting point when comparing it with another system is to see if it can supply some particular quality that is needed for the work in question. Look at the purpose and function of the work, and see if screen printing can provide something that another printing system cannot. For example, if you are making an outdoor metal sign, then screen printing can produce it in a durable, high-gloss enamel, which can be baked for maximum resistance against the elements.

You may want to use screen printing for printing light colors on dark backgrounds, even white on black. Or you can use it for printing fluorescent colors, metallics, or wherever powerful, rich hues are needed. It is also used for applying the adhesive for flocking and for clear varnish overprint applications. High-gloss, UV-cured, clear varnishes, applied by screen printing and dried in a fraction of a second straight from the press, are economical substitutes for laminating. (For more on finishing methods, see chapter 14.)

Another important advantage of screen printing is that it takes to a much wider range of surfaces and materials than any other system. And whatever the material is, the technology of screen inks is now so far advanced that compatible inks are always available, along with detailed information on their use and qualities.

Before considering limits in reproduction definition, whether of fine lines or halftone dots, an essential point must be understood: although screen printing can be applied to various rough, irregular surfaces, this advantage is limited to relatively coarse work. When used for fine detail, screen printing is extremely sensitive to bad surfaces. This means that for high quality in fine-line or halftone work, a smooth surface is essential.

A good screen printer should be able to print a four-point type size, including the complete lower case, to a high standard of quality on a suitable surface. A specialist can print type as small as two-point on a good surface, with no filling-in of small counters (called "centers" by screen printers), such as the island portion of the lowercase *e*. This degree of quality, as yet not a standard in commercial screen printing, is better than in letterpress, which because of its squash-edge is not good at reproducing very small type.

Essentially, the ability to print a good monochrome halftone is the first basis for good color reproduction. Given the required printing standards, successful four-color work is then a matter of the separation and color-correction techniques, followed by proper transparency balance of the four process inks used by the screen printer.

How to Use *7* Flexographic Printing

Flexography is short on history but long on technology. While it has a distant ancestry tracing back to the 1860s, the process as we know it today was born in 1905 with an aniline press built by an Alsatian, C. A. Holweg. It combined three elements that have characterized the process throughout its spectacular development: (1) use of a rubber plate; (2) use of dyes instead of traditional printer's ink; and (3) operation in combination with a machine so that packaging can be printed and assembled in the same operation.

Although flexography serves many purposes today, it is still closely associated with several kinds of packaging. Indeed, rubber plates were first adopted in order to print corrugated boxboard.

History of Flexography

An examination of flexography's roots reveals a fascinating example of how closely printing is interwoven with general history. Modern packaging began with the logistics of feeding the huge Union armies of the Civil War. Food was preserved in tin cans, which were packaged in wooden boxes. The slats that made up such boxes were printed and debossed by letterpress. This wood was fed lengthwise into the first "longway presses," whose descendents today are flexograph presses that print relatively long and narrow substrates.

Eventually, corrugated board replaced wood. Because the heavy stamping impression of wood printing today would break down the corrugations, only the lightest "kiss impression" is required. Among other changes, the engraved brass plates used on wood have been replaced by flexible rubber ones (in Germany the process is still called *gummidruck,* or "rubber printing").

Not until the early 1920s did the process become widespread in the United States. It was then called "aniline printing" because aniline oil was the basic substance used to synthesize the coal-tar dyestuffs that pigmented the inks peculiar to the process. But aniline became a bad word as the public—rightly or wrongly—associated coal tar with toxicity. In the 1940s, with the packaging of almost all foods that previously had been sold in bulk, fears arose, unwarranted as they may have been, of contamination by these inks. It became an obsession of the industry to find a new name, cleansed of the alarming implications of aniline. In 1952, "flexography" was adopted by the Packaging Institute Forum, again demonstrating the symbiosis between that industry and flexographic printing.

While resiliency of plates (now as often made of photopolymer as of rubber) remains an identifying characteristic of flexography, the most significant element in the process today is the "anilox roller" that meters the ink applied to the printing plate. But the anilox is a relatively recent development and can best be understood by examining the basic process.

Principles of Flexography

Flexography, like letterpress, is a relief printing process. In its earliest days, its rubber printing plates could not hold detail. That was no problem, though, since such printing was performed on coarse surfaces where fine detail not only was unnecessary but might even have been inappropriate. The inks then used were extremely fast drying, and this still holds true today. Many characteristics of flexographic inks are shared with those used in rotogravure; the two processes also share a mechanical device, the "doctor blade." In both processes the blade controls the amount of ink applied to the printing plate and then to the printed surface, the substrate. (For more on gravure printing, see chapter 5.)

In conventional letterpress (see chapter 4), very viscous ink comes from a tray and is carried by a series of small rollers—the "inking train"—to a larger one that actually inks the printing plate. The many rollers are necessary to ensure that ink is applied to the plate in exact amounts for a good reproduction. If various areas of the plate—those with large halftones, heavy reverses, simple type—require differing amounts of ink, adjustment is made by changing the flow of ink from tray to first roller in the train. Offset lithography (see chapter 3) uses the same inking train and viscous inks.

In rotogravure, an intaglio printing method, the image is incised into a copper roll. Very thin inks are used, close cousins in viscosity to flexography's. Roto presses have no inking trains. The printing cylinder, carrying millions of tiny cups, or wells, incised at varying depths, rotates into an ink fountain. The cups fill with ink, which naturally covers the surface of the plate as well. As the copper cylinder emerges from the fountain, its surface is scraped with the doctor blade, a thin strip of steel or some plastic material. This rubs the ink off the surface but leaves the cups filled. As they are pressed against the paper web by an impression cylinder, the ink transfers to the paper. The deeper the well or cup, the more ink is deposited and the darker that portion of the image.

In flexography a single inking roller turns through an ink fountain and delivers a relatively generous amount of ink to the anilox roller (see figure 7-1). The anilox, made of metal or ceramic, is completely covered with incised, gravurelike wells, varying in number from 80 to 500 per linear inch. The doctor blade, made of spring steel or

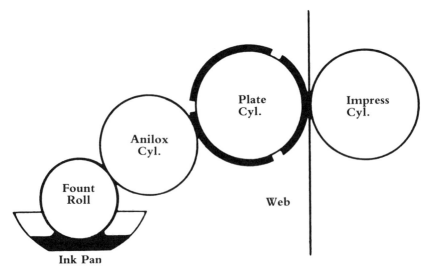

Figure 7-1. The setup of the apparatus for flexographic printing.

phenolic material, clears the surface of ink and assures that only the measured ink in the cups will be applied to the printing plate. That amount can be measured far more precisely in the cups than when a layer of ink is carried on conventional rollers.

Like the gravure printing plate, that of flexography is also curved by wrapping a flexible plate around a cylinder. It is natural that flexography be a rotary-printing process. Its beginning as a printer of packaging materials dictated the process, and such materials are almost always in rolls.

There are variations. The anilox roll may turn through the ink fountain, eliminating the fountain roller. Or an applicator may pump ink from the fountain onto the anilox roll. But they do not affect the basic function of that anilox roll, which is to deposit a finely controlled amount of ink to the printing plate.

Flexographic Printing Presses

There are four kinds of flexographic presses, and all are rotary. The "stack press" arranges individual color-printing units one over the other; some technical (but insignificant, practically) advantages accrue from such an arrangement. The "central-impression cylinder press"—also called the drum, common-impression, or CI press—has a single large-impression cylinder around which are arranged all the printing stations. Such an arrangement maintains close register of all color plates, because the web is supported by the impression cylinder. This eliminates possible sagging between stations that distorts the length of the substrate and, of course, the images previously printed on it. The "in-line press" arranges its printing stations horizontally, as is common with conventional letterpress presses. Almost unique to flexography are "narrow-web presses," using web widths of only 4 to 24 inches, most usually 6-inch, 8-inch or 10-inch widths. These produce labels, tags, tickets, and so on, and almost always are combined with a die-cutting process to cut the printing to shape. These presses also perforate, slit, and sheet the web or rewind it while maintaining register.

All these presses can—and occasionally do—have capacity for almost unlimited numbers of stations. Most usually there are six, adequate for process-color work plus metallic printing or varnishing.

Because the plates are light, because the desired kiss impression requires no heavy-impression cylinders or great pressure, and because the inking train has been eliminated, flexographic presses are relatively light and can attain high speeds. Narrow-web presses customarily operate at 650 feet per minute; larger presses have been clocked at 2,000 feet per minute.

Flexographic Printing Plates

The rubber printing plate that pioneered flexography remains in use today, although significant improvements have been made. Making the flexographic plate parallels the stereotyping of letterpress plates. It all starts with two-dimensional art or phototype. From this flat material is made a relief photoengraving in zinc or magnesium or, when finest detail must be held, in copper.

From the photoengraving—or three-dimensional hot-metal type— is made a matrix of cellulose and thermosetting resin. (Asbestos fibers may be added to reduce the shrinking of the matrix, which distorts the original image.) This material is molded under heat and extreme pressure around the three-dimensional original and makes a mirror mold of that original. From this matrix, which can be reused almost indefinitely, is "cast" the printing plate of natural rubber or a number of synthetic materials, including Buna N, Neoprene, isoprene, butyl, and vinyls.

After the rubber has been poured into the matrix, it cures for about 10 minutes at 307°F. Because it is so thin, the rubber plate must be stripped from the mold with great care while it is still hot; otherwise it will tear. The plate is then affixed to the press cylinder with double-backed sticky tape. Or the plate may be permanently vulcanized, during the molding operation, onto a thin sheet of metal. This assures greater dimensional stability of the plate for fine color work. The rubber-metal plate is fastened to the press cylinder with pins or by magnetism. Nylon and polyesters are also used for backing the rubber and stabilizing its dimensions.

Using photopolymers, a quite recent development, creates the relief printing plate in one operation. It also eliminates making the photoengraving and the matrix, both steps requiring costly time, materials, and labor. The polymer may be in a sheet borne by thin aluminum or plastic, or it may be in liquid form. In either instance, the process begins with a negative of the image to be reproduced.

As light passes through the negative onto the plastic, areas exposed to light are hardened. The unexposed polymer, still soft, is washed away with water and detergent, a much simpler and safer method than etching the background away with photoengraver's acid. The resulting relief image is at least semiresilient, the original characteristic of the method entitling it to the first two syllables of flexography.

By using liquid polymers, the platemaker actually manufactures the photosensitive sheet. Onto a bearing sheet of metal or plastic, liquid polymer is flowed to the desired depth. In color and viscosity, the polymer looks like honey. The negative of the original copy is exposed onto this newly created sheet, and the process proceeds as it did using sheet polymer. Just-washed plates are swollen, almost mushy, and tacky. Oven drying, under closely controlled temperature and time, eliminates swelling and the distortion thus created, hardens the plate, and removes the stickiness.

One aspect of the liquid process disturbs some observers. Because the polymer is still semiliquid and hot as the negative is exposed, there can be no contact between the plastic and the film, lest the latter be dissolved. Although the space between the two is minute, there is still some diffusion of light before it hits the polymer; with it comes a distortion of the image. This is so slight it cannot be detected by looking at a single type character, for instance, even with a magnifying glass. But many craftspeople discern an overall mushiness to the printed page that discomforts them.

Flexography and the Packaging Industry

True to its beginnings as the printer of packaging materials, flexography maintains close ties with the packaging industry and the material it uses. Paperboard and corrugated paper, with which flexography really began, remain a staple. These materials require sheet-fed printing, of course, but continued press improvement enables quite high speeds. Printers and designers alike are trying to raise the quality of printing on these papers. Despite considerable success, however, paper cartons still stress utilitarian rather than highly decorative printing.

It is with newer packaging materials that flexography really comes into its own. This began with the introduction of cellophane in 1930. It was an almost ideal wrapping but, by letterpress and offset, almost impossible to print on. Totally unabsorbent and transparent, it demanded new inks and techniques. The inks had to adhere to this slippery surface, and heat was required for permanent adhesion.

All this happened at the very nadir of the Great Depression, when printers had little money for capital investment, so a great deal of do-it-yourself press modification took place. Because the only inks that would work on cellophane were dyestuffs as transparent as the substrate, there was little contrast between image and background, and printing was far less than vivid. Overprinting was impossible, and that kept designs quite simple.

An opaque aniline ink was necessary, and in 1931 the first, simple white, was perfected. White was used both for providing a background for surprinting and to add to dye inks to make them opaque.

As so often happens, the solution to one problem brought new problems. Existing presses often had as few as 10 or 12 inches between printing stations. If overprinting was to be done, inks could not dry sufficiently in this space, even though the top printing speed was a relatively sedate 150 feet per minute. Nor was there adequate space for heat-drying units between stations. When heaters were used, they were so close to the ink supply that the ink dried and caked on rollers, necessitating frequent press stops to clean them off. The real solution was new press design. But it was the introduction of cellophane that caused many significant strides to be made in flexography.

Cellophane remains a popular substrate, but many other film wrappings also account for huge volumes of printing—polyesters, polyethylenes, and the many vinyls among them. Their printing demands high craftsmanship. Many are dimensionally unstable, so that register is a constant problem. All of them have surfaces that are most inhospitable to ink.

Aluminum foils are highly practical packaging materials, and they also afford possibilities for striking, sales-persuasive design. Here, transparent inks are at an advantage, as they retain and even enhance the brilliance of the metal. As aluminum is rolled down to the .001-inch thickness of common foil, some lubrication is required between the metal and the rollers. Even the slightest trace of this lubricant will prevent adhesion of ink to metal. Annealing is supposed to evaporate all the lubricant, but often traces still remain. The foil is therefore wash-coated with substances such as shellac, which not only provides a good printing surface but fills in tiny pinholes that occur when metal is rolled to such thinness. That extremely light gauge makes it difficult to roll the foil through the press without wrinkling or without web breaks. Thus, craftsmanship on the press must be high.

Laminated materials grow in popularity as special packaging needs cannot be met by a single material. Sometimes a single ply is printed by flexography, then laminated to another material. Or the already-joined plies are printed. Because laminated materials are quite expensive, controlling waste becomes a most important factor in the printing process.

Preparing Materials for Flexography

For the typical user or buyer of flexographic printing, the many technicalities of this process can safely remain just that: technicalities best left to the printer. As with conventional letterpress and offset, the buyer need only make the simple decisions of stock, size, and color of ink. But flexography does require some modification in the preparation of mechanical paste-ups and, indeed, in artwork itself (for more on these general topics, see chapters 8 and 10).

The designer who prepares copy for flexography will, in most cases, be working with packaging and will be familiar with the special requirements of this medium. Packaging materials have inherent qualities—the brilliance of foil and the transparency of films—that can be exploited for point-of-purchase appeal (see chapter 1).

The designer should be familiar not only with flexography generally but with the equipment to be used on any given job. Central cylinder presses, for instance, can hold closer register than can the other two presses. Die-cutting and similar processes (detailed in chapter 14) may, in specific instances, be more or less efficient, depending on the basic design of the printed piece. As with any printing process, the designer is wise to consult with the printer, platemaker, and other purveyors before beginning the design of any job that is the least bit out of the ordinary.

The major factor a designer need consider is the distortion that occurs with flexographic plates. If molded plates are used, they may shrink appreciably, the extent determined by the materials used. The vertical stretching that occurs when the plate is wrapped around the cylinder will affect not only the overall repeat length of the design but the placement of various elements within the design. Circles and squares are most noticeably elongated. To complicate things, a plate with relatively small copy blocks will both shrink and stretch at a different rate from one with large solids or reverses.

As if that were not enough to keep the designer honest, the substrate often has dimensional instability. This makes fine register difficult or even impossible to maintain. Another problem can come from the transparency of ink. Overlapping areas of transparent inks may create a new color, unlike overlapping opaque inks that appear black.

Register is a continuing problem that is better avoided than solved. Hairline register, which requires an overlap of a trifle more than a point—$\frac{1}{62}$ of an inch—requires maximum accuracy of art, engraving, plates, cylinders, and press—and superior craftsmanship of the pressman. In most instances, it is dubious whether the desired results are worth the cost entailed. Butt register, in which adjacent colors meet exactly, with no overlap at all, is even more difficult to achieve.

For most jobs, commercial register with a $2\frac{1}{4}$-point overlap is usually satisfactory and affords adequate tolerance through the art-to-printing process. Even easier to achieve is overprinting, which can be said to require no register. A happy fringe benefit is that many attractive visual effects are produced by this method. Machinery attached to flexo presses for fabricating packaging (cutters, slitters, creasers, folders, the whole catalog) have liberal tolerances. The designer had best avoid placing copy near corners or where slight misregister may hide copy under the sealing area.

Common sense and a familiarity with the processes involved will prevent most of the problems even before they occur. A major safeguard is a test plate run on a proof press. Comparison of printing to original art will indicate the compensation needed for plate shrinkage and stretch, as well as resulting distortion of elements, especially squares and circles.

That plate will also reveal the optimum sizes and weights of type, especially in body sizes and in reverses (although the wise designer will only reluctantly reverse body type in any circumstance). Optimum screens of benday (patterns of lines and dots) and acetate shading sheets can also be shown in test plates.

Testing can be refined by using two plates. One would carry large areas of solids and various reverses. The other would carry small masses of type with large nonprinting areas. Both test plates should have measured gradations running the entire length and width of the plate. Half-inch tick marks work well, although smaller increments may also be used. This device will not only show total distortion but will indicate whether shrinkage or stretching is uniform throughout the plate. A series of squares and circles will show distortions. Mechanical screens should be shown in densities of 30 percent to 60 percent and in the lines-per-inch most frequently used for the designer's work; 65-line, 85-line and 100-line screens will probably be all that are consistently needed.

The ultimate test, of course, is the finished job. Each flexographic project should be filed with a complete summary of all pertinent information (indeed, this is good advice for any printing job). This includes the kind of press, inks, and substrate—not only material but any special washing or coating it received; the amount of compensation for distortion; the material used for plates; whether molding from matrix or direct negative-to-polymer processes was used; and so on. The more information that can be preserved, even if it seems insignificant at the moment, the better the designer can master the versatility of the flexography process.

Simplicity of design—a basic virtue—is never more beneficial than in creating layouts for flexography. It is always desirable; when it helps avoid production problems, it is an additional reward.

The future of flexography is certainly bright. From the crude rubber-stamp image on rough carton paper, the quality of the process has improved so that today the finest four-color work is possible with screens as fine as 150-line. Press speeds constantly increase as web scanners can check register at high speeds. Improvement in polymers is immediately translated into better plates or more effective methods of making them.

As with other printing processes, experiments are being conducted with lasers by the flexo industry, which has several national and international associations dedicated to, and active in, research and development as well as promotion.

With the exception of the era of letterpress's incunabula, no facet of the printing industry has seen such far-reaching improvements in a single lifetime as has flexography. One can only attempt fascinating predictions for the next lifetime.

Preparing Artwork 8
for Reproduction

No matter which printing method you choose, the successful production of a printed piece depends greatly on the careful preparation of the various graphic elements. After the copy has been written, edited, and typeset; after photographs have been taken, developed, and printed; and after artwork has been executed, all of this material must be assembled and readied for the printer. Short of discussing the following step of preparing paste-ups (the subject of chapter 10), this chapter will explain how the graphic elements are prepared.

Design Layouts

Although the graphic designer (or graphic artist or art director; the synonymous terms vary) may be involved from the very outset of a printing project, it is at this point that he or she begins to bring everything together. The designer starts by producing a rough visualization of the printed piece and then progressively improves and expands this graphic plan. These visual representations are called the layouts, of which there are three types: (1) thumbnail sketches; (2) rough layouts; and (3) comprehensive layouts.

The *thumbnail,* as it is generally called, is a simple sketch, drawn in proportion to but smaller than the final piece. It loosely shows where the type, photographs, and art will be arranged on the page. Its details are few, so once the idea is there, the thumbnail can be drawn in a matter of minutes. Usually the designer renders several thumbnails, each depicting an alternative approach to assembling the same graphic elements.

After the thumbnails have been reviewed, one or a combination of several progress to a more detailed, actual-size sketch, called a *rough layout,* or simply a *rough.* The rough presents a more complete visual sample, although actual type and art are not yet included. In some cases, the rough may be adequate enough for paste-up to begin.

If the layout's complexity demands an even more detailed representation, however, the designer will produce a *comprehensive layout,* or *comp.* Unlike the thumbnail or rough, the comp can include set type (normally "dummy" or "Greek" type and not the actual typeset copy), headlines, photos, and illustrations, as well as detailed notes, instructions, and other design specifications. For this reason, considerable expense may be incurred in preparing a comp.

Large or complex projects, such as books, catalogs, and other multipage publications, might require comps in order to gain approval from those involved, in order to begin paste-up.

Assembling Copy

After the layouts have been prepared and approved, the designer is ready to begin assembling the copy elements for paste-up. Printers generally refer to three types of copy: (1) line copy, (2) continuous-tone copy, and (3) full-color copy.

Line copy or *line art* is any copy that will print solid, either in black or color. This includes typeset copy (text, headlines, and captions), charts, diagrams, and line drawings or illustrations. The latter may be pen-and-ink, brush-and-ink, pencil, or charcoal renderings. Also in this category are various kinds of tints and shadings employed as design elements. Line copy also includes type surprints, where type is overprinted on a background color or tint, and type reversals, knockouts, or dropouts, where light type is printed on a darker background.

Continuous-tone copy refers to tones of light and dark that combine to produce graphics. A black-and-white photograph is probably the most common form of continuous-tone copy. Such copy contains a gradation of tones, from nearly white to nearly black, and all shades in between. Color photos, artwork, and shades or tints can also fall into this category. *Full-color copy* is discussed later in this chapter.

When preparing line copy, the designer should make certain that the typeset matter, charts, drawings, or other material is of proper density to print clearly; unless deliberately chosen for effect, no breaks, nicks, or other imperfections should go through that would make the printed piece appear faded or chipped.

Continuous-tone copy, especially in photo form, requires a screening process in order to be printed. This process, referred to as halftones, is explained in chapter 4.

Preliminary Planning

Even before the actual preparation of line and continuous-tone copy, the designer can make things easier by preplanning before the art is drawn or the photograph is taken. The designer should let the artist know what printing method is going to be used, the size that would reproduce best, what kind of paper is best for the printer (see chapter 11), and other information that will eliminate timely or costly work later.

If a photographer is used, the designer may want to specify a certain type of film to use or request that prints be of a certain size. He or she may want to see a contact sheet even before prints are made. Again, anything that can be done in these preliminary stages will save time and money with the printer, who may have to make up for mistakes before the piece goes on press. There can never be too much preplanning.

After receiving acceptable art, type, or photographs, you may still want to alter them for design purposes. For instance, different kinds of halftone screens can create effects to enhance design. A photo can be made more "contrasty" (lighter lights and darker darks), or it can be retouched or airbrushed to add or delete certain elements; it is also possible to silhouette a halftone to drop out certain background elements or to isolate one or more parts of the photo. All these factors can be determined before the paste-ups are done.

Two-Color Printing

Before examining how to prepare full-color art, we should consider two-color printing, which is really a manipulation of continuous-tone copy in either photos or artwork. Subtle yet effective use of two-color printing can be an inexpensive way to add color and vitality to a finished product.

A second color can be added by way of a background shading or tint over which type is printed. Also possible is a two-color photograph, called a duotone. This involves actually making two negatives of the photo; usually one is color and other is black. A "fake" duotone can also be printed by simply printing the halftone over a color background.

Four-Color Process Printing

Full-color copy involves four-color process printing of artwork or photographs. To accomplish this, three colors of partially transparent, primary-color inks are added to black to reproduce any colors, typically on white paper. Most color printing is produced with the four-color process, although a fifth color may be added at considerable expense.

The three process colors are cyan (blue), magenta (red), and yellow. By using certain combinations and percentages of these three colors, together with black, full-color printing is possible. For example, a certain mixture of red and blue reproduces a purple; red and yellow reproduces orange; and so on. Thus, partially transparent inks are used on the printing press to create solid colors.

The graphic designer works with two types of full-color copy, *reflection copy* and *transmission copy*. Reflection copy is produced on an opaque material, such as paper or board, and reflects light. This includes color photographic prints, paintings, drawings, and illustrations. Transmission copy allows light to pass through it. This includes photo transparencies and slides.

In order to print either reflection or transmission color copy, the piece has to be color separated to produce negatives of the three process colors and the black color. This job usually falls to an outside supplier, the color separator. The separator uses machinery that scans the color copy and electronically or photochemically separates the colors and their relative densities. Laser-based separations are also used. In any case, the separator should supply you with a printed proof that can be color corrected if necessary before producing the four-color negatives for the printer.

Four-color separations and printing mean added expense to the project, so special care should be taken in preparing color copy. If you are going to use an outside color separator, there are several steps you can take to ensure satisfactory work and to cut down on preparation (and added cost) at the printer.

Preparing Color Copy for Separation

Before sending color to the separator, certain portions of the piece can be cropped, or the piece itself can be enlarged, or reduced. Instructions can either be marked on the copy with a grease pencil, or else stats can be made (to size, and pasted on mechanical layout boards) of the prints or transparencies. This latter method can help avoid any questions the separator might have involving sizing and lets the separator know exactly how and where the color appears on the page. In addition, if you plan to add process color to the headlines or type, you can put the typeset copy right on the mechanical. This way, one set of negatives can include all the type and illustrated materials for an entire page.

If there is more than one piece of color copy on a single page or two-page spread, it is possible to assemble them together for a "gang" separation. Typically, the separator will charge a base rate for a single separation on the page, with each additional element separated at minimal cost.

Generally speaking, acceptable separations can be made from either reflection or transmission color copy. Keep in mind, however, that if submitting transparencies, the larger the format the better. Thus, an 8-by-10-inch transparency may produce a clearer, sharper separation than a 35-mm transparency. And to avoid trouble, try not to submit transparencies in any type of paper, plastic, or glass mounts; they will just have to be cut into to make the separation. It is best to have some sort of plastic protective sleeve to put the transparencies into for the separator.

Tips on Handling Artwork

No matter what kind of copy you are working with—line, continuous-tone, or full-color—certain steps can be taken to avoid mishandling by the paste-up artist, the color separator, or the printer.

1. This should perhaps go without saying, but always strive for the best possible quality in the execution of the art or photography. Make sure your instructions are precise and complete before work begins.

2. Always label copy before it is sent anywhere. Clearly indicate the job name or number, the page it will appear on, and possibly a brief description of the copy (the name of the person photographed, for instance). Keep a written record of what material you have sent out, when it was sent, to whom, and when it is to be returned. You might even want to make a photocopy of any material before releasing it.

3. Avoid writing directly on photos and artwork, if possible. Instead, prepare an acetate or tissue overlay on which to write any identifications or instructions. Use a grease pencil or felt-tip pen; stay away from sharp pencils and ball-point pens. Never write directly on the surface of the material, if possible, even on an overlay.

4. Never stack photos that have been written on, front or back; ink marks on photographs are not only frustrating, they are sometimes permanent.

5. If you are mounting color copy to be separated, avoid using a heavy board or other surface. Separators usually put the material on a cylinder when the color is scanned, so the mounting surface cannot be too stiff.

6. Always include explicit instructions to whoever is receiving the material, so as to avoid questions, confusion, and ultimately errors. If you are unsure of anything, call the person you are working with and ask your questions before you send out material.

If you plan carefully and prepare copy according to the printer's specifications, the chances of success are much greater. The many ways to manipulate graphic elements can give any final printed piece an effective and appealing look.

Typography 9

Communication, via the written language, has never advanced with such rapidity as in this century. From primitive Egyptian scrolls, dating back to 3500 B.C., to today's satellite transmissions of news directly to computers and laser printers, it all began with the invention of the alphabet. It is this system of letters, as translated into type, that is the subject of this chapter.

As is the case with any tool, centuries of repeated experimentation has brought about an evolution of the alphabet. From primitive scribblings to today's highly efficient, computerized systems of typographical design, the symbols of this familiar configuration now convey not only thoughts but moods and feelings as well.

A History of Type

Ancient Egyptians combined pictographs and pictographic syllables into expressive symbols. These symbols were then borrowed and improved on by the Semites. By 1000 B.C., the Phoenicians had taken the alphabet, to which they added new symbols to express vowels, to other parts of the world. Cypriots began to use the alphabet, and then Greeks, who made still further improvements. By A.D. 124, the Etruscans, who had learned the alphabet from the Greeks, introduced it in Italy, where the Romans adopted it.

In all this time, the evolving alphabet was written in capital or uppercase letters. Finally, Roman scribes improvised a lowercase alphabet as a means of conserving writing space, and Roman stone-cutters developed the art of carving letters into stone, which led to further refinement and actual styles of type. Angular serifs were added to the vertical strokes to cover imperfect stroke endings.

Until the mid-1400s and the inventions of Johann Gutenberg, most writing was done with brush strokes. The development of movable metal type and the printing press by Gutenberg and his colleagues caused communication of the alphabet to become fast, precise, and practical, thus ushering in a blossoming of the art of printing.

Soon a variety of typefaces was introduced, many of which remain as standards in the industry. Beginning in 1464, when the first roman letterform was cast into type in Germany, Italian, French, and English typographers established variations of the widely used roman typefaces. Parisian Claude Garamond gave us the Garamond face, grouped into the family known as *roman old style*. William Caslon, an Englishman, developed Caslon Old Style. Then, in 1788, Italian printer Giambattista Bodoni drew roman letters with thin and sharp unbracketed serifs. His Bodoni typeface marked a transition to *modern roman* styles (see figure 9–1).

When it comes to acting excellence, 13-year-old Alyssa Milano is her own boss. For two years, she's done a great job with her role as Samantha on ABC's hit TV series *Who's the Boss?* Last summer, Alyssa turned in a commanding performance in Commando, the blockbuster movie starring muscleman Arnold Schwarzenegger. And as this issue's cover girl, she's smashing!

a

When it comes to acting excellence, 13-year-old Alyssa Milano is her own boss. For two years, she's done a great job with her role as Samantha on ABC's hit TV series *Who's the Boss?* Last summer, Alyssa turned in a commanding performance in Commando, the blockbuster movie starring muscleman Arnold Schwarzenegger. And as this issue's cover girl, she's smashing!

b

When it comes to acting excellence, 13-year-old Alyssa Milano is her own boss. For two years, she's done a great job with her role as Samantha on ABC's hit TV series *Who's the Boss?* Last summer, Alyssa turned in a commanding performance in Commando, the blockbuster movie starring muscleman Arnold Schwarzenegger. And as this issue's cover girl, she's smashing!

c

Figure 9-1. Samples of several variations of roman typefaces: (a) Garamond Roman; (b) Caslon Old Style; and (c) Bodoni Roman.

Mechanical Typesetting

The next great accomplishment in typesetting was the invention by Ottmar Mergenthaler of the Linotype machine in 1886. This machine, which eliminated the slow and tedious method of setting movable type by hand, had a typewriterlike keyboard that activated a system of casting hot lead from brass matrices into continuous lines of type; thus the term *hot type*. The framed type was used on a flatbed press for direct, relief printing,—letterpress—or to emboss a heavy paper matrix into a mold to form a semicylindrical lead plate called a stereotype. The Monotype machine, which also set type in lead, was later developed. (For more on letterpress printing, see chapter 4.)

Cold Type

In the 1940s, a new technology began to take root, a simple form of composition that became known as *cold type*. This "strike-on" method utilized a carbon-paper ribbon, through which a metal font of type left its imprint on a sheet of paper.

In 1948, Ralph C. Coxhead developed the Verityper, a redesigned typewriter with interchangeable fonts or series of type. The type was arranged in sizes of 6, 8, 10, and 12 points, a point (pt.) being $1/72$ inch. It was Coxhead who, in comparing his method to that of setting type in hot lead, coined the term *cold type*.

After the copy was composed on paper, it was retyped and justified, which meant it was aligned at both left and right margins. The copy was then ready to be "pasted up" on paper boards called mechanicals (see chapter 8 for more on preparing artwork and type for reproduction). The chief advantages of this process were simplicity, economy, and speed, all of which became important with the advent of offset lithographic printing (see chapter 3).

IBM helped advance cold typesetting in the 1950s with its PSM (Proportional Spacing Machine) electric keyboard device. This was followed by the Justowriter, which used paper tape and two typing units in a technique that was considered revolutionary. A unit called a recorder generated perforated paper type, with justified lines and a hard-copy printout. The tape was then fed into a second reproducing unit, which finally produced justified copy ready for paste-up.

Phototypesetting

Through technology, the Justowriter evolved to produce type by photographic techniques, which have come to dominate typesetting today. The principle behind so-called photocomposition is the high-speed projection of characters through a film type-font onto photographic paper or film. Elements such as length of typeset lines, type sizes, and paragraph indentations are recorded on magnetic tapes or disks with the use of a conventional keyboard.

Such keyboards were initially designed with the above-average typist in mind. Apart from the already-familiar "qwerty" keyboard layout, they included new keys to relay functional commands to the typesetting machine. There was no carriage to hold hard copy. All typing was "blind," in a continuous string of words and commands, and sorted out by the machine's computer.

Tape-producing keyboards are essentially punching machines, transmitting coded keystrokes to tape. Those keyboards, sometimes referred to as "unintelligent" or "idiot" machines, produce raw type; "intelligent" machines, engineered with a memory, produce type ready for paste-up. The memory is mounted on a removable printed circuit board; its programmed commands activate the many functions of the typesetting machine.

As the development of the keyboard progressed, important innovations were introduced. Most dramatic was the addition of a CRT (cathode ray tube). This allows the typesetter to edit copy—from transposing paragraphs to correcting misspelled words—on the CRT before the type is actually set.

It is also possible to view and edit an entire, multipage job on the CRT, one page at a time, by entering the proper code into the typesetting machine. Improved magnetic memory disks permit even quicker and more accurate access to the stored material. An 8-inch floppy disk can store approximately 256,000 characters on one side, or nearly the contents of a paperback novel. And a rigid, or hard, 14-inch disk can store up to 44 million characters per side.

In order for the machine to execute its digital commands electronically, it also has built-in, permanent software to control such functions as line justification, copy indentation, and leading between lines, as well as usage and spelling dictionaries.

A modern phototypesetting machine will set type in sizes ranging from 4 points to 72 points by simply having the proper code entered into it. Some have built-in, digital type-fonts; each character is programmed to reproduce the design and relative dimensions of the type style called for by the operator. There is no film font but rather a projection of pinpoint dots emanating from a strobe light to form the actual character. Thus, the number of moving mechanical parts used to effect type change is eliminated, and greater readout speeds are achieved.

Once the paper or film has been exposed, it rolls into a cassette or light-proof magazine and is taken to a developing processor. A good processor will develop, stop, fix, wash, and dry a galley as it is fed through its cycle. The end result is a photographic rendition of a typeset galley, ready for proofreading and paste-up.

There is nothing worse in composition than pasting up a page with more than one density of black type, as shown in figure 9–2. Therefore, a standard of black, once reached, must be maintained, and certain quality standards must be observed. For example, the temperature of the developing chemicals must be kept at a maximum daily average of 68°, and the strobe lights exposing the film or paper must be kept at the same intensity.

Word Processing

The latest technology in typesetting is the word processor. These desk-top units are becoming affordable enough so that companies of almost any size are able to generate a wide range of printed materials in-house. Without computer-programming training, a typist can produce multiple copies of "personalized" form-letters, for example, or a "clean" manuscript on a memory disk, which can be fed directly into a phototypesetting machine.

Word processing is such an important factor in printing and production that it is covered in detail in chapter 16.

Typesetting Specifications

Once the copy is ready to be typeset, it must be marked with certain specifications or instructions for the typesetter to follow. This is often referred to as "speccing" type or copy. Such specifications include the font of type to be used, the width of the typeset columns, and

When it comes to acting excellence, 13-year-old Alyssa Milano is her own boss. For two years, she's done a great job with her role as Samantha on ABC's hit TV series *Who's the Boss?* Last summer, Alyssa turned in a commanding performance in Commando, the blockbuster movie starring muscleman Arnold Schwarzenegger. And as this issue's cover girl, she's smashing!

a

When it comes to acting excellence, 13-year-old Alyssa Milano is her own boss. For two years, she's done a great job with her role as Samantha on ABC's hit TV series *Who's the Boss?* Last summer, Alyssa turned in a commanding performance in Commando, the blockbuster movie starring muscleman Arnold Schwarzenegger. And as this issue's cover girl, she's smashing!

b

c

Figure 9-2. Samples of type developed with uneven density of black: (a) overexposed type; (b) underexposed type; and (c) normal type.

the leading or spacing between individual lines and/or paragraphs. Very often a publication, company, or organization follows a predetermined style of type specifications.

Depending on the source of the copy, different people may be responsible for speccing the type: sometimes it is the author or the copy editor, other times it is the designer or layout artist; under certain circumstances, the task can be handled by the typesetter.

Marking copy with type specifications should cover a number of elements:

• Type style or styles to be used for specific components of the copy, including body type, major and secondary headline type, subheads or running headlines, and quoted material.

- Type point sizes for each of these components.
- Column width of copy, headlines, or quoted material.
- Leading or spacing between lines of text, paragraphs, or headlines and paragraphs.
- Indentations of text, headlines, and subheadlines.

Figure 9–3 shows various samples of type-speccing marks.

After the specifications have been determined, the copy is marked in a code that the typesetter will understand. In the case of computerized phototypesetting, the specifications are coded at the beginning of each new job, onto the machine's memory tape or disk. This initial coding is called the *parameters* of the job.

For example, the coded entry may read [M35.6 A02 L14.0 P10]QL. Translation: measure (or width) 35 picas, 6 points; style 02 on A drum; leading 14 points; point-size 10; then quad left. During the keyboard operation, the type style, line length, and leading commands can be changed at the beginning of each line where changes are required.

A device to call up stored information in a typesetting machine is called the *format*. The format is used to reduce and facilitate the typing of combinations of procedural instructions to the typesetting machine. For example, a format can be used to call up complex and detailed instructions such as indentations, setting mathematical equations, and changes in type-font styles and sizes.

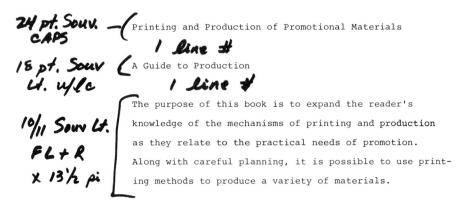

Figure 9-3. Samples of type-speccing marks.

Type Measurements

Type and space between copy on typeset pages are universally measured in points (pts) and picas. There are 12 points to a pica and approximately 6 picas to the inch. Generally, machine-set type can come in sizes ranging from 4 to 72 points. When indicating point sizes, one is referring to the height of the type, or, in other words, the dimension from the top of the ascender to the bottom of the descender of the character.

No matter how tall the capital letters or the body of the lowercase of a typeface may be, one still measures from ascender to descender. But be aware that type designers sometimes exaggerate letters in many popular styles in order to create diversity in layout styles. One such design is the Helvetica typeface, a modern sans serif design, with shortened ascenders and descenders, as shown in figure 9–4. Notice that the measure again is taken from the top of the ascender to the bottom of the descender. Yet the body size of Helvetica is actually about 1 to 2 points larger than its point size would indicate.

For example, an 8-point Helvetica has a body as large as a conventional 9- or 10-point type. Therefore, one can set more lines of type on a page without sacrificing the readability of the type. And, as is shown in figure 9–5, an opposite effect can also be achieved. The designer has used this type for a decorative, feminine style that would be appropriate for, say, a cosmetics advertisement.

The width of type is measured in units. Most of today's typesetting machines set type on an 18-unit basis. For example, the capital letter *M,* on an 18-unit basis, will take up the entire width, while the letter *N* takes half the full width, or 9 units. This accounts for the terms

When it comes to acting excellence, 13-year-old Alyssa Milano is her own boss. For two years, she's done a great job with her role as Samantha on ABC's hit TV series *Who's the Boss?* Last summer, Alyssa turned in a commanding performance in Commando, the blockbuster movie starring muscleman Arnold Schwarzenegger. And as this issue's cover girl, she's smashing!

Figure 9-4. This sample of sans serif Helvetica type is actually larger than its point size would indicate.

When it comes to acting excellence, 13-year-old Alyssa Milano is her own boss. For two years, she's done a great job with her role as Samantha on ABC's hit TV series *Who's the Boss?* Last summer, Alyssa turned in a commanding performance in Commando, the blockbuster movie starring muscleman Arnold Schwarzenegger. And as this issue's cover girl, she's smashing!

When it comes to acting excellence, 13-year-old Alyssa Milano is her own boss. For two years, she's done a great job with her role as Samantha on ABC's hit TV series *Who's the Boss?* Last summer, Alyssa turned in a commanding performance in Commando, the blockbuster movie starring muscleman Arnold Schwarzenegger. And as this issue's cover girl, she's smashing!

Figure 9-5. Another variation of sans serif type displays a feminine, decorative style.

em space and *en space,* or *em dash* and *en dash,* referring to space between characters.

The space occupied by the characters is called *set space.* The typesetter, according to the designer's wishes, can adjust the size of the set space by simply programming this information into the typesetting machine. In this way, the terms *tight-space* or to *set copy tight* have crept into today's typesetting jargon. The terms refer to setting the type so that each character practically touches the next, as shown in figure 9–6. In hot-metal typesetting, this technique is called mortising and requires the physical cutting away of the blank space on the edge of one letter so that the next one fits snugly next to it.

The space between lines of type is called *leading* (rhymes with *heading*), a term borrowed from the hot-lead typesetting technique of widening lines of type by inserting thin strips of lead between them.

The strips are precisely cast in thicknesses of a half point or more. Therefore, to "lead" copy by one point means to insert one-point lead strips between each line of type.

When it comes to acting excellence, 13-year-old Alyssa Milano is her own boss. For two years, she's done a great job with her role as Samantha on ABC's hit TV series *Who's the Boss?* Last summer, Alyssa turned in a commanding performance in Commando, the blockbuster movie starring muscleman Arnold Schwarzenegger. And as this issue's cover girl, she's smashing!

Figure 9-6. A sample of type that has been set very tight.

In phototypesetting, lines of type are opened up by rollers carrying the film type-fonts, much as a typewriter platen carries paper to the next space and next line of type. The leading between lines is first addressed in the parameters of the job as a command code, entered into the typesetting machine just before the actual manuscript is typeset. Any changes in leading during the job will require new commands to be entered into the computer.

Unlike metal typesetting, which by its physical nature restricts the space between lines of type, phototypesetting involves no restriction in leading. One line can run into another, or even be superimposed on the preceding line. Indeed, the flexibility in spacing in photocomposition has given designers a tremendous opportunity to exercise artistry.

Advanced, computerized typesetting machines have the added spacing capabilities that allow layout specifications to be performed during the actual typesetting. For instance, if a page calls for several columns of type to be set with various widths between them, such commands can be programmed into the machine. Furthermore, with the aid of the CRT, such a layout can be previewed on the screen before the type is set and pasted up.

Selecting Type

In the past, selecting an appropriate type style for a particular job was generally the typographer's lot. Traditionally, typographers spent many years working with a wide variety of typefaces and were usually master typesetters themselves. Their craft was in selecting a body type that suited the job and complementing it with the right headline typeface. Secondary headlines and other components were usually selected from the same families or fonts of type. For example, serif body type was never coupled with sans serif headlines. And since the medium was bulky metal type, time-consuming changes of typefaces were kept to a minimum. Even something as seemingly simple as italicizing a word or phrase meant stopping production completely to change heavy type magazines.

In contrast, phototypesetting machines are capable of carrying up to 18 type-fonts and can change typefaces with the touch of a button. Consequently, mixing and matching typefaces and sizes no longer requires much of an expenditure. Today's art director or layout designer—yesterday's typographer—is freer to experiment with type as a design element, without having to incur higher costs.

Another obvious advantage in selecting cold type is the ease of storing memory tapes and disks, especially if a reprint is desired. Likewise, this makes it easier to maintain print projects that demand periodic updating, without the time and expense of resetting type. For example, if a company needs to mail extensive lists of products whose prices fluctuate regularly, the typesetter can "call up" the previous-run job on the CRT and merely input the appropriate changes.

When it comes to selecting the right typeface for a job, literally thousands of styles and families of type are available, broken down into four general categories: roman (or serif), sans serif, script, and black test. Figure 9–7 illustrates several examples of each.

a

When it comes to acting excellence, 13-year-old Alyssa Milano is her own boss. For two years, she's done a great job with her role as Samantha on ABC's hit TV series *Who's the Boss?* Last summer, Alyssa turned in a commanding performance in Commando, the blockbuster movie starring muscleman Arnold Schwarzenegger. And as this issue's cover girl, she's smashing!

c

When it comes to acting excellence, 13-year-old Alyssa Milano is her own boss. For two years, she's done a great job with her role as Samantha on ABC's hit TV series Who's the Boss? Last summer, Alyssa turned in a commanding performance in Commando, the blockbuster movie starring muscleman Arnold Schwarzenegger. And as this issue's cover girl, she's smashing!

b

When it comes to acting excellence, 13-year-old Alyssa Milano is her own boss. For two years, she's done a great job with her role as Samantha on ABC's hit TV series *Who's the Boss?* Last summer, Alyssa turned in a commanding performance in Commando, the blockbuster movie starring muscleman Arnold Schwarzenegger. And as this issue's cover girl, she's smashing!

d

When it comes to acting excellence, 13-year-old Alyssa Milano is her own boss. For two years, she's done a great job with her role as Samantha on ABC's hit TV series *Who's the Boss?* Last summer, Alyssa turned in a commanding performance in Commando, the blockbuster movie starring muscleman Arnold Schwarzenegger. And as this issue's cover girl, she's smashing!

Figure 9-7. Samples of four categories of type: (a) roman, serif; (b) roman, sans serif; (c) script; and (d) ultrabold roman, sans serif.

Naturally, a designer can choose type to reflect a particular mood or feeling of the printed piece. Some styles of body type provoke certain feelings by their rough, bold look, while very much different moods can be captured with the use of light, delicate type. Some type styles can transport the reader to a certain part of the world or a particular time in history. One type style can impart a sense of urgency; another, a sense of dignity. Thus, the designer's job—to capture a prescribed feeling—can involve type as well as photographs, charts, or decorative rules and lines.

The same principles hold true when choosing headlines, which serve to attract the reader to the copy. Some heads shout for attention, while others are designed to be unobtrusive and blend with the rest of the copy.

The strict rules of the past about matching body type and headlines have been broken by today's schools of design, which allow much more mixing of type families and styles. Nonetheless, certain aesthetic guidelines are still generally followed: heads should be of similar or heavier weights than body type, using boldface or even just a larger-size version of the body type; and mixing script faces with others is usually to be avoided, as it tends to look out of place (the same applies to mixing black text with other faces). On the other hand, wide use of sans serif heads with roman body type has been successful, as have different families of type mixed in body type.

Justification and Hyphenation

Another design element affected by type is justification. While most copy is justified on the left-hand margin (with the exception, of course, of paragraph beginnings and other indented matter), a non-justified or "ragged" right-hand margin is sometimes used. There are also instances in which ragged copy is practically a necessity, as when setting type in narrow column widths; in this case, justifying the copy may create unsightly gaps between words.

Ragged type can also be used if you want to avoid the use of hyphens at the end of lines completely, although most phototypesetting machines can automatically hyphenate words. Keep in mind, however, that the use of too many hyphenated words at the end of lines can be confusing to the reader, so for the sake of readability as well as aesthetics, avoid excessive hyphenation. The accepted rule is to not exceed three successive hyphenations (another command that can be programmed into the typesetting machine).

Copy Fitting

Very often, type is set to fit within specified widths and depths or around a photograph or other graphic element. Therefore, typesetters have devised methods to translate typed manuscript pages so the copy fits into the space allotted by the designer. In some cases, when the layout is determined first, the precise number of lines of copy needed, including the number of characters per line, can be assigned to the copywriter.

Layout design is the subject of chapter 8, but here we will provide some examples of copy fitting that should be included in our discussion of type.

A typical illustration of copy fitting is to run copy around a photograph in a one-page promotion piece. Two columns are each designed 20 picas wide, with the photo positioned flush to the right margin, at the top of the right column. The photo is reduced to 7 by 10 picas. Now, the space for the photo, plus a margin below and to the left of it, must be calculated.

The design calls for a 1-pica margin to the left of the 7-pica photo—or 8 picas—which leaves a width of 12 picas for copy. Using a 9-point type, which measures approximately 3.0 characters per pica, the 12-pica lines will accommodate 36 characters per line. A 1-pica margin is also designed below the 10-pica photo, along with another 1-pica line for the caption, for a total of 12 lines.

The 9-point type is to be set with 11 points leading between each line. Convert the 12-pica depth into points (remember, there are 12 points per pica): 12 picas × 12 points = 144 points. Then divide 144 points by 11 points, the measure of the leading, to equal 13 + lines of 12-pica width.

Finally, instruct the typesetter to set the first 13 lines at a 12-pica width and to set 20-pica lines beginning with the 14th line. (Note: if the photo is positioned on the left side of the column, simply instruct the typesetter to program the machine to indent each of the first 13 lines by 8 picas.)

Sometimes print advertising calls for the type to be literally wrapped, or contoured, around an irregularly shaped photo. This can be a laborious, trial-and-error exercise for the typesetter, who must calculate each line individually. But again, computer-aided phototypesetting machines can greatly accelerate such tasks.

Layout Design and Paste-up

Once the copy has been typeset and the galleys have been proofread, the job is ready to be designed and pasted up on mechanical layout boards (more on this in chapter 8).

It is at this stage that headlines, lined rules, and other type components that enhance a layout can be added. This is also another area where computer-aided typesetting machines are replacing manual methods. Many of today's advanced machines can be programmed to reproduce lined rules; display type, such as main and secondary headlines, can be set on specially designed equipment.

Preparing 10 Paste-Ups for Reproduction

In order to ready all the copy elements—typeset text, line art, half-tones, and so on—for the printing process, a paste-up, or mechanical, must be prepared. On it, all the above copy elements are affixed in the exact position in which they will appear in the final printed piece.

Preparing the mechanical or paste-up is a step-by-step process that follows the design of the piece. A paste-up or mechanical artist is normally employed. Many techniques are used to create various visual effects, and special tools and materials are often needed.

Following is a review and explanation of the process. You will most likely want to refer to chapter 8 for information on preparing art elements for reproduction, since this is included in the paste-up process.

Words on Paper

Direct Position

Composing copy in position, using the typewriter or a "strike-on" composer, eliminates the need to "paste up" composition on a base sheet. For example, type a letter on a letterhead and use the complete page as the original for duplication. Narrative composition, some statistical presentations, and certain types of business forms can be prepared directly camera-ready.

Composing copy in position using phototypesetting equipment requires detailed mark-up (or speccing) and planning so that words and rules will set in position when the composition appears on the photo paper or film, which will be the "original" for platemaking or copying.

Generally, it is found that some paste-up is essential to achieve camera-ready pages, what with illustrations, screened halftones, shading, corrections, and alterations.

While it is helpful to compose words on paper in position, there must also be an efficient method to paste composition in position to create or alter a camera-ready page.

Paste-up Technique to Prepare Mechanical Art
Composition is prepared, either by strike-on or phototypesetting, to create type lines on strips of paper in lengths suitable for trimming and pasting in position on a base sheet or mechanical (see figure 10–1). Words might be typed to cut and paste on business forms, in column strips suitable for publication paste-up, or in paragraphs for a brochure. The composition should always be prepared to allow for the simple placement of type areas. For example, a block of statistical type within a brochure should be set as a complete unit. (For more information on typography and typesetting, see chapter 9.)

Typesetting vs. Typewriter Composition
Phototypesetting equipment produces images of proportionally spaced characters, with the narrow letters taking up less width than the wide ones. The uppercase letters *I, J,* and *T,* for example, take up less space than do the lowercase *a, b,* or *c.* The letters *W* and *m* take up more space. Therefore, when type is set on typesetting units, more characters will fit per horizontal inch than in typewriter composition, where all characters are equally spaced at 10 or 12 characters per inch.

The cost of proportional typesetting should be equated with words per page of typewriter composition versus the increased words per page of typeset, which also has the flexibility to produce bold, italic, and type-size changes.

Headlines
The typographer can keyboard headlines in larger sizes along with the text typesetting output. However, headlines may also be set on a "headline setter," such as the Strip Printer and Kroy (figure 10–2).

Figure 10-1. Base sheet or mechanical on which paste-ups are done.

The Strip Printer uses a film strip of type characters. The film is moved to the desired letter and exposed in position onto a strip of photo paper, which is subsequently processed. The Kroy uses a type disk, which is rotated to the desired location and each character contacted to a strip of adhesive-backed paper.

Dry-Transfer Type and Self-Adhesive Cutout Lettering
Rub-on transfer type can be affixed to practically any surface to produce sharp lettering. An advantage of dry transfer is that it can be placed directly onto screened halftones.

Acetate, self-adhesive lettering is cut out with an art knife, lifted, and put in position. Many attractive hand-lettered and standard type styles are available, in sheet form, for application.

Basic Steps to Preparing Mechanical Art

• *Prepare a printing plan on grid paper.* Making up a layout or planning the location of copy elements on a sheet of paper is most easily performed on grid paper. Grid lines, printed in light nonreproducible

Figure 10-2. Strip Printer headline setter.

blue, are perfectly visible, yet pencil lines show up boldly. The grid squares make it easy to space margins and column gutters and to generally place pictures, illustrations, and headings. Grid paper is a time-saver, especially when it is printed with a scale framing the outside border area. You eliminate the need to continually pick up a ruler and measure. If a base sheet that matches the grid paper is used for the paste-up, this final assembly will be faster and easier.

Pica grid paper allows for a logical and helpful grid increment of measure: a ⅙-inch vertical and horizontal spacing, or six spaces per inch, the equivalent of standard typewriter vertical spacing. For example, ruling a business form with horizontal lines drawn every other space will allow efficient use in a typewriter set on double-space carriage return.

Therefore, type that is set 14 picas would occupy 14 squares of this grid paper in width, and type that is set 12 points would occupy one space vertically, since each pica is 12 points high. (It is acknowledged that there is a minute difference between a pica and ⅙ inch, but it is so fractional it is not a problem in paste-up preparation.)

Those who are in the habit of working in inches will find little difficulty switching over to pica measure.

• *Adhere the composition and other elements to a base sheet.* Wax or rubber cement may be used to apply a coating of adhesive on the back of all material to be pasted up. The pieces can then be placed on vinyl cutting-board backers.

• *Tape a preprinted, bordered base sheet (sometimes referred to as a mechanical board) to your work surface* (explained below in "The Board System").

• *Draw any required guidelines on the sheet with a nonreproducible-blue pen or pencil.*

• *Draw any rules (these will reproduce) required with a technical pen containing dense black ink.*

• *Trim, position, and burnish the elements.* Cut apart the copy elements, using a hobby-type knife and straightedge, while they are still on the cutting board (see figure 10–3). Lift the cut pieces off the board and position them on the base sheet. Finally, square-up (align) and burnish (tack down) the copy to assure proper adhesion to the sheet.

• *Proof.* Make a photocopy of the mechanical to submit for approval and/or alterations.

Figure 10-3. Using an art knife to cut apart a galley of type before paste-up.

The Board System

Acrylic Paste-up Boards

A working surface consisting of a clear acrylic paste-up board, along with a lightweight T-square, offers a convenient setup for preparing paste-ups (see figure 10–4). A base sheet (mechanical) may be taped, top and bottom, to the board surface. Copy may be aligned using the T-square. Vertical and horizontal lines can be ruled by turning the board to any position.

A standard acrylic paste-up board measures 11¾ by 15¾ inches, with a ⅜-inch thickness and is precision milled on all sides. Because it is clear, it may be placed on a light table, used as an aid to position copy. A positive plastic grid is useful to place on the board beneath the base sheet. The light shows through the paper, thereby accentuating the grid's lines, which will help in aligning copy elements both vertically and horizontally. This technique is particularly useful when laying down columns of type for publications or narrative copy on pages. The T-square can also be used to check alignment and rule, and to trim copy. The paste-up board provides flexibility and convenience, since it sits atop a desk, art table, or light table.

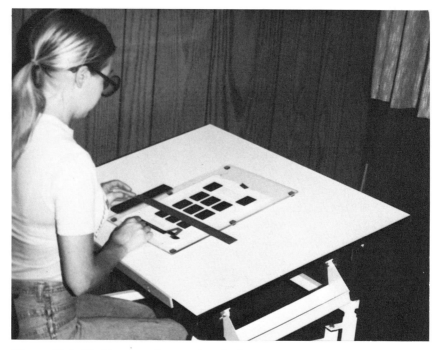

Figure 10-4. Working on a drawing board, the artist uses an acrylic paste-up board and a lightweight T-square.

T-square

A light, thin-steel T-square is ideal for quick maneuverability when its head is pressed firmly against the edge of the acrylic paste-up board. The blade can be used as a cutting guide and ruling edge. The thin blade close to the paper allows for precise, visible alignment of type proofs and corrections.

Grid Cards for Paste-up

A grid card, printed in nonreproducible-blue ink, is also a useful base sheet when pasting down copy, especially if special guidelines are unnecessary. (When blue line planning is required, use the border base sheet.) Grid cards are available in a variety of increments, including the suggested pica grid, which matches the grid planning paper. Printing planned on the grid paper is later pasted down on the grid card for quick, efficient preparation.

Adhesives

Today's most popular adhesive for pasting up copy is wax. It is applied to the back of paper with either a hand waxer or a motorized mechanical waxer (see figures 10–5 and 10–6). These units contain heating elements to melt a special wax adhesive. After waxing, the copy is placed on a backer or cutting board for final trimming with an art knife. Copy can be easily lifted from the cutting board to place on the base sheet. Pointed tweezers are ideal for picking up bits and pieces to control the placement of waxed copy.

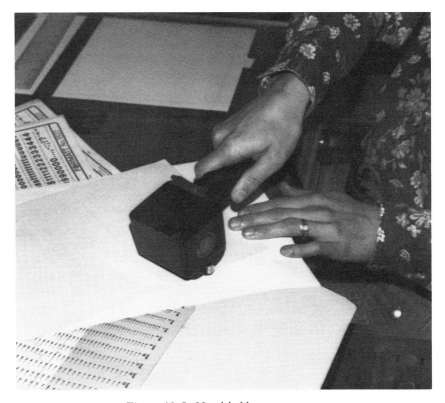

Figure 10-5. Hand-held copy waxer.

Figure 10-6. Mechanical copy waxer.

Wax is a clear, clean adhesive. It does not deteriorate; it allows repositioning, and makes it possible to adjust copy with the tip of a knife point to its precise location. To ensure good adhesion, waxed copy must be burnished carefully, typically with a hand-held roller, to secure it firmly to the base sheet (see figure 10–7).

Other adhesives often used for paste-up preparation include rubber cement and spray adhesive, sold in pressure-valve cans. Rubber cement is still widely used, although it does tend to get a bit sloppy, especially if copy has to be picked up and repositioned several times during paste-up. And, as with the spray adhesives, unpleasant fumes can be a detraction.

The newest form of adhesive is a pressure-sensitive material, placed on the back of the copy. The copy can then be either rubbed onto the paste-up or run through a special machine that applies pressure and adheres the copy to the paste-up.

Figure 10-7. A hand-held copy burnisher helps secure galleys of type to the paste-up board.

Border Tape

Border tape is used to apply reproducible lines and borders on such printed pieces as advertising, sales literature, charts, and graphs. Rolls of tape are available in attractive varieties of designs and rules. To place border tape on a paste-up, draw position lines in blue and apply a length of tape by stretching it taut and pressing the guideline with the thumbs. Dab the tape lightly for proper adhesion, since a heavy burnish could cause the line to wave.

Some tapes will allow for the mitered-corner technique of trimming. Allow the corners to overlap about one-half inch, miter-cut the corners as though you were making a picture frame, and lift off the excess pieces, as shown in figure 10–8.

Preparing Mechanical Art for Photographs

Prescreened Prints

Photographs and artwork can be prescreened to size on photosensitive paper for placement directly on the mechanical, to reproduce in com-

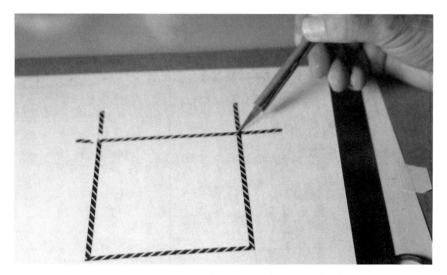

Figure 10-8. Applying and cutting a decorative border tape.

bination with the line copy (text). The prescreening is usually accomplished using a diffusion transfer print or Photo-Mechanical Transfer, PMT (the Kodak trade name), print.

There are certain advantages to this method: the screened print can be positioned directly on the mechanical, cropped, and combined with typeset copy; the paste-up may be photocopied for approval, which often can eliminate the need to produce a silverprint to show the customer a complete page proof; the need for a film halftone is eliminated, thus reducing material and labor cost.

The Window

"Windows" on mechanicals, indicating photos, are created by placing a red or black patch in the same size and position where the photo will print. Some printers will prepare windows themselves. When exposed to light, the patch will appear as a clear area on the film negative; hence the term *window*. The film halftone is fastened on the window to combine the halftone with the line negative as one piece. A window can be produced by taking the following steps:

1. Determine the area of the original photograph you want to use, and rule thin crop-marks in the marginal areas of the print.

2. If the photo needs to be reduced, use a proportional scale (explained later), to set scales on height and width of cropped area. Note the reduced height and width.

3. Rule a light outline of the halftone area on the paste-up.

4. Place a piece of red pressure-sensitive blockout film on the outlined area, with the red extending beyond the outline.

5. Use an art knife and straightedge to cut through the film layer on guidelines visible through the translucent red film.

6. Peel off the excess film around the perimeter of the photo to form the red window.

Do not place type closer than ⅛ inch from the edge of a window, since it may become distorted or bolder due to the extra thickness at the halftone's edge.

Stats or Prints
The need may arise to enlarge or reduce line art to a size to fit directly on a paste-up. A litho camera or stat camera will produce a suitable print on photo paper. On the art, mark the reduction required by using a nonreproducing blue pencil or pen. Outside stat houses or typesetting firms can also provide this service.

Reducing and Enlarging
Illustrations, photographs, and pages may need to be reduced or enlarged to achieve a desired width. The height will also reduce proportionately.

To do so, draw an outline of the original on a sheet of tracing paper, and then draw a diagonal line from the lower left corner to the upper right. Next, measure the reduced width and draw a perpendicular line at that point. The point where the perpendicular bisects the diagonal indicates the height after reduction. A proportion dial or wheel is a device that will quickly calculate the final reduced dimension when the original dimension is set on the dial (see figure 10–9).

The Reverse
A reverse is an image in which the black and white areas have been exchanged with those of the original subject. Generally, it is a white image on a black background, used principally as a design element. A reverse is created from an original by producing a film positive,

which is then contacted to print paper to make a reverse print. This reverse can then be applied to the mechanical.

If the reverse print is not large enough to fill the reverse area on the paste-up, you can apply a red blockout film-patch on the paste-up. Then affix the reverse atop the red patch in position. Red and black will photograph equally on litho film and photo-direct plates.

The Overlay

An Overlay Prepares for a Second Color or Tint.

An overlay, a transparent sheet placed over a mechanical, separates additional mechanical art for color, line, or halftone material from the copy on the mechanical (see figure 10–10). One must be sure that whatever is placed on the overlay registers with the art on the mechanical.

Figure 10-9. A proportion wheel is used to size photos.

Figure 10-10. Applying an acetate overlay to indicate shading on a chart. Special care must be taken to keep the overlay "in register."

In this way, the camera operator can produce two separate negatives, one of the base and one of the overlay, by shooting a negative of the mechanical; then inserting white paper between the overlay and the mechanical; and finally shooting a negative of the overlay.

Whatever is ruled or placed on the overlay will photograph separately. The transparency of the overlay material allows you to view where to position your elements to register in relation to the base. A polyester or acetate plastic sheet is good overlay material; the polyester is stable and will not stretch or shrink.

For overlays prepared for printing large areas or intricate close-register, a peel-off type of overlay masking film will be easier to manipulate (see figure 10-11). This film has a peel-off membrane coating and is available in transparent red and amber. Either the red or amber will photograph on camera, but if you cut an overlay to contact directly on film, be certain to use the red. If you have several overlays, use red for one and amber for the other to see the difference in the color patches.

Ruling the Film Overlay

It may prove helpful to ink rule lines on an overlay in correct position relative to the composition on the mechanical. The rules are thus completely separate from the mechanical, yet both may be photographed in combination, either on photo-direct plates or on film.

To prepare the ruled overlay, use a treated polyester type of film that is receptive to inked ruling with a technical pen. The overlay can be secured to the mechanical by using a pin register system or by hinge taping the overlay material over the mechanical with white paper tape. The overlay will hold secure register with the mechanical.

Use a technical pen with ink specially formulated for ink ruling on film. You will obtain dense black rules on the film.

Technical Pens for Ruling

The technical pen provides excellent quality ink rules on paper or film. The lines will be consistent with the size of the tube point of

Figure 10-11. Cutting an amber overlay to indicate shading or color on an illustration.

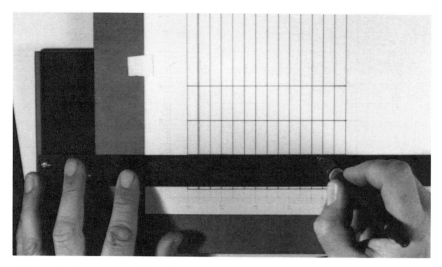

Figure 10-12. Using a technical pen to draw rules. The pen should be held vertically.

the pen. Very thin hairlines or thick bold rules can be ruled with a minimum of practice.

The pen should be held vertically; draw slowly, with very light pressure, to produce consistent rule density (see figure 10–12). It is important to use the proper ink in the pen so that correct and consistent ink flow can be expected. For some ruling work, a fine black ballpoint pen may be useful, if care is taken to prevent a slight blot when beginning to rule a line.

Basic Tools for Preparing Mechanical Art

While many tools and devices are available, the following are basic to the preparation of paste-ups:
• *Paste-up board and T-square.* A milled board provides a convenient surface for the mechanical. The companion T-square is used to align copy pieces at the edge of the board.
• *Art knife with a no. 11 blade.* This type of knife is required for trimming and cutting paper and film.
• *Tweezers.* These are convenient for picking up strips of paper to place on the mechanical, as shown in figure 10–13. Pointed tweezers

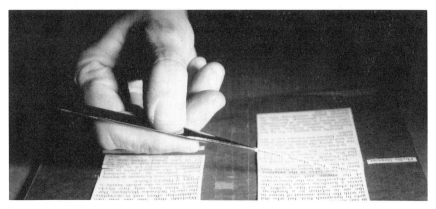

Figure 10-13. Tweezers can be used to pick up and apply small strips of type.

are best, as they can be used closed, to adjust or straighten a piece of copy prior to burnishing.

• *Burnisher.* A burnishing stick or roller will help affix copy to the base sheet to assure firm adhesion.

• *Graham color-coded centering rule.* Words, lines, and copy blocks must be centered on the mechanical, and this special rule helps in quickly locating the centers (see figure 10–14).

• *Nonreproducible blue pen and pencil.* Using one of these, marks can be drawn or ruled on the mechanical as reference points for the place-

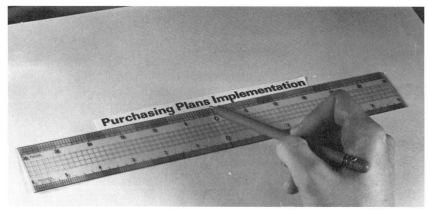

Figure 10-14. A centering rule is used to center a headline.

ment of copy. The lines need not be erased, since they will not photograph or copy.
• *Technical pens.* Several pens of various line widths will allow for drawing camera-ready rules as required.

Other Helpful Tools, Supplies, and Equipment

Triangle	Compass	Plastic grid
Cutting boards	Graphic white	Scissors
Proportion dial	Art brushes	Red blockout film
Line gauge	White paper tape	Amber/red peel-coat
Cutting guide	Waxer	film
Dividers	Light table or box	

Selecting **11** *Paper*

If you have the ultimate responsibility for selecting the paper that will be used for a printing job, you are in an enviable position. You play a major part in creating the impact a printed piece will have.

Paper plays a subtle yet important role in creating the effectiveness of the final printed piece. Selecting the right paper for the job is not an easy task. There are so many colors, textures, brand names, and other practical considerations to be made that it is sometimes difficult to know just where to begin.

In order to become more familiar with the wide selection and variety of papers, it will help to examine the different general categories of papers that are on the market.

Uncoated versus Coated Papers

A basic decision will be whether the job requires a coated or uncoated paper surface. A coated paper surface is one on which a coating formulation has been applied in order to smooth out the paper's natural hills and valleys, visible under a microscope. Coating applied to paper polishes the surface and makes it even smoother and glossier. Coated papers can be made to be nonreflective (dull), slightly polished (glossy), or very highly polished (cast-coated).

One reason to select a coated paper is to provide a smooth, level surface for reproducing halftones. The precise reproduction of the halftone dot is better suited to coated paper than uncoated paper.

Uncoated papers do not have coating applied to their surface and therefore are rougher in texture. Although they still can be made smooth by supercalendering (polishing), this smoothness does not approach that obtained by putting a film coating on the surface. Uncoated papers do permit halftone reproduction but not for fine, precise reproduction. Uncoated papers are generally used for reproducing line illustrations and/or typeset matter. The many uses for both coated and uncoated papers will help in your selection; the job itself, as well, will dictate which to use.

Types of Coated Papers

Following is a chart (see figure 11–1) of various coated papers and a comparison of their different surfaces. This in turn is followed by a listing of the various types of coated papers available.

Matte-coated Papers

These are coated but not supercalendered after the coating operation. They provide a pleasing background for typeset and/or halftone material and are especially useful if you do not want a highly reflective surface or if large areas of typeset material are to be reproduced.

COMPARISON OF PAPER SURFACES

	Uncoated Offset	Matte Coated	Dull Coated	Gloss Coated	Cast Coated
Bulk	High	Medium	Low	Low	Low
Surface Smoothness	Uneven, Broken	Uneven	Level/ Smooth	Level/ Smooth	Ultra-smooth
Surface Reflectance	No Glare, Somewhat Mottled	No Glare, Grainy Appearance	Uniform Reflectance, No Glare	Glare, Uniform Reflectance	Extreme Glare, Uniform Reflectance
Texture	Fairly Rough	Somewhat Smooth	Smooth	Smooth	Very Smooth
Ink Characteristics (Receptivity)	Uneven	Somewhat Uniform, Still Somewhat Mottled	Uniform Smooth	Uniform Smooth	Uniform Smooth

Figure 11-1. Chart of coated papers, and their different surfaces.

Dull-coated Papers

Coated and then specially supercalendered to provide a very smooth yet nonreflective printing surface, these papers are slightly better for reproducing halftones, while providing a pleasant nonreflective surface for typeset matter. This type of paper is used often for annual reports.

Gloss-coated Papers

Used for all types of sales literature and publications, these have been coated and then polished to a shiny, high-gloss surface by a super-calendering process at the paper mill.

High-gloss Papers

Very highly polished, with a mirrorlike surface, these papers allow excellent halftone reproduction on a highly reflective surface. They are often used for very fine-line screen reproduction because of their ability to show precise detail.

Embossed-coated Papers

These coated papers are embossed, in a range of patterns, to create a textured effect on the surface of the paper.

Types of Uncoated Paper

Many uncoated papers are available as well. Generally, uncoated papers are well suited to such pieces as menus, annual reports, brochures, booklets, letterheads, and envelopes, among dozens of others.

One of the major features of uncoated paper is its availability in many colors and textures. Mills will often make different hues of different colors, and ofter a wide range of textures, further expanding your creative selection process.

Below are some of the uncoated papers available:

Text Papers

This term refers to papers used for the text of a booklet or brochure; it can also mean that the paper is textured.

Antique-finish Papers

These are bulky, uncoated papers with a rough, distinctive, textured surface. They reflect little light and are a good choice for printed materials with heavy type coverage. Their relative bulkiness provides them with a feeling of richness and quality, which can add a great deal of character to the printed piece.

Felt-finished Papers

This terminology refers to papers on which a pattern has been imprinted by a felt on the paper machine. While not as rough as antique paper, it still makes for a very distinctive, bulky, quality sheet of paper. Felt-finished papers are used for annual report covers, fancy menus, brochures, booklets, folders, and posters.

Machine-finished Papers

Machine finish, or MF papers as they are sometimes referred to, are similar to antique paper surfaces but are smoother and more polished. While their smoothness makes them capable of providing a surface for halftone reproduction, they are more often used for reproduction of line art.

Supercalendered Papers

These are highly polished, having been passed through alternating steel-and-cotton or steel-and-paper supercalendering rolls after being made. This supercalendering operation smooths and levels the paper, giving it a better surface for printing reproduction.

Laid-finish Papers

This special-finish feature provides a pattern of vertical and horizontal lines on the finished sheet. These lines are put onto the paper by wires attached to a special roller, a "dandy roll," which is on the paper machine. A laid finish gives a very distinctive and readily identifiable mark to the paper. It is often used for stationery, invitations, prestige brochures, and other printed pieces where high quality and distinctiveness are desired.

Embossed-paper Finishes

Embossing patterns are applied to the paper after it has been taken off the paper machine. A large number of embossing patterns are available that can help create even more interesting effects for a printed piece. Embossing the surface is accomplished by passing the paper between two rollers, one of which stamps the pattern into the paper. This process is then repeated on the other side of the paper. Embossed finishes can enhance brochures, posters, menus, magazine inserts, and folders.

Inexpensive Papers

Other grades of paper, including bond, index, tag, and newsprint, offer good reproduction quality of text and halftones at a lower cost than coated and uncoated stocks. Here is a list of these papers and some of their uses:

Bond Papers

These are characterized by good strength and erasability and are available in a wide range of colors. They are used extensively for inexpensive letterheads, sales fliers, brochures, product sheets, and other commercial printing applications where the quality of a textured or coated paper is not required or budgeted for. They are manufactured by many paper mills and stocked by almost all paper merchants throughout the country.

Index Papers

Generally made from rag-content papers in heavier weights, index papers are used when strength and durability are necessary. Many manufacturers offer these in tinted pastel colors for use in the business-form format.

Tag Papers

These are similar to index stock, but are not made from rag stock and so are less expensive. Tag stock is usually stronger, and more often used in industrial applications where strength and durability are essential.

Newsprint

Just as the name describes, this is used principally to print newspapers. Newsprint comes in a variety of quality levels, but is basically the least expensive printing paper available. It contains a large percentage of groundwood fibers and is subject to a great deal of yellowing, fading, and eventual deterioration. Newsprint is available in a variety of lighter weights, too, and is occasionally used as a novelty paper for printing promotional pieces (see chapter 1).

Types of Cover Papers

Cover papers are another area in which there is a great variety of selection. Cover papers are heavier-weight versions of book-weight paper, regardless of whether they are coated or uncoated. They extend one's flexibility because their uses, while limited somewhat, can offer a new dimension to a printed piece. Cover papers afford the strength for folding numerous times, die-cutting, and unique scoring applications (see chapter 14). Following are some of the cover papers you may consider:

Coated Cover Papers
These are heavier-weight versions of regular coated papers and can be used for matching cover applications as well as by themselves for folders, sign cards, and posters.

Neutral-pH Cover Papers
These are acid-free, which makes them long-lasting. They are usually used for fine-art print reproduction, since they have a resistance to yellowing and aging. Many of them are buffered with calcium carbonate, which actually reduces the acidity of the sheet to pH 7.0, or neutral acidity.

Cotton Content Papers
These are noted for their superior strength and flexibility and are excellent for scoring, folding, deep embossing, hot stamping, and die-cutting.

Embossed Cover Papers
These can create unusual textured patterns that can simulate canvas or other creative finishes in a deeper pattern than would be possible on regular book-weight papers.

Duplex Papers
These specialized papers are really two sheets pasted together to form a thicker, more durable sheet. The pasted sheets must be of the same basis weight but can be of any number of color combinations. Unusual and effective graphic techniques can be achieved with die-cutting, folding, and scoring duplex papers for such applications as folders, invitations, menus, covers, and fliers.

How to Find Out More about Papers

Paper manufacturers offer a wide variety of materials to help in your selection of paper. Most paper mills are represented by independent paper merchants, whom you can readily locate in the Yellow Pages of your telephone directory. These merchants can become valuable friends when it comes to selecting paper.

Within many paper-merchant organizations will be at least one person who devotes the majority of his or her time to working with advertising agencies, design studios, and other creative agencies that regularly prepare printed materials. These specialists are usually knowledgeable both in advertising design and in varieties of paper. They can provide you with sample sheets, dummies, mill-produced promotional materials, printed samples, and other items that will make paper selection easier and more complete. In addition, you will learn which papers are readily available in your market and which will have to be ordered from the mill and therefore not be available to you as quickly.

Other excellent sources of information about paper are printers' salespeople. They generally know a great deal about varieties of paper and availability, as well as the printing processes you will be using. Whenever possible, get to know printers' salespeople and use their knowledge to help you.

Following are some of the materials that you should find helpful in learning more about the varieties of papers available to you:

Sample Books

Paper mills produce sample books (see figures 11–2 and 11–3), show a particular grade of paper and provide as much information as possible about that paper. Sample books include information on stocking, as well as availability of colors, sizes, basis weights, and whether a particular grade has matching cover stock and envelopes available. The sample book will also note any special ordering information unique to that grade of paper. Many times sample books provide samples of selected finishing techniques, such as blind embossing, hot stamping, or die-cutting. Some books will even feature four-color reproductions to show that the paper is suitable for four-color reproduction. Sample books are made available by the paper mills to their merchants, who can pass them along to paper specifiers.

Figure 11-2. (Left) Paper-mill sample books are an excellent source of information about a particular grade of mill paper. They contain samples of colors, textures, various weights, and special grade information.

Figure 11-3. (Right) Mill sample books sometimes use special graphic techniques to demonstrate how well their papers perform. This particular sample book shows four-color reproduction on the front cover.

Comprehensive Paper Selectors
Many mills offer a comprehensive paper selector (see figure 11–4), which incorporates all the grades manufactured by that particular mill and gives stocking and availability information on each of the colors and grades. Paper merchants, too, have recently started providing comprehensive paper selectors of all of the papers that they stock locally. Since paper merchants represent many paper mills, their paper selectors are quite extensive, and many times include information to give you an idea of the comparative costs of one paper versus a similar one. Try to obtain selectors from several merchants in your marketing area, so you will have an idea of what is available locally.

Figure 11-4. Comprehensive paper selectors are available from both paper mills and paper merchants. These selectors can help you select colors and textures and will also tell you about paper availability in your market area.

Layout Portfolios

Layout portfolios (see figure 11–5), or "designer kits," as they are sometimes known, provide a larger-size sample sheet (usually 12½ by 19 inches) which can be used to make layouts and working dummies. They are most useful after paper selection has been made and can be obtained from local paper merchants.

Paper Dummies

If you need larger sizes of sample sheets than can be provided by the layout portfolio, most paper merchants maintain a sample department and can provide full press-size sheets of the particular paper you wish to use for a job (see figure 11-6).

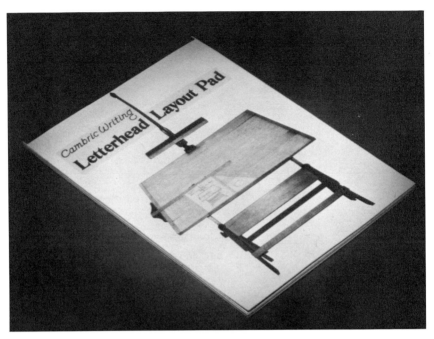

Figure 11-5. Layout pads are available from paper mills through their local merchants and are excellent sources for working-size papers for artists and production people.

Figure 11-6. Plain samples and dummies are helpful after a paper selection has been made.

Figure 11-7. Commercially printed samples are an excellent source of ideas about paper usage and selection.

Printed Samples

Sometimes paper selection can be made easier by having access to a variety of printed samples of similar jobs (see figure 11–7). Most mills and many paper merchants can supply you with such samples. For instance, if you are seeking paper ideas for an annual report, you can review a variety of existing annual reports that have been printed on various papers. These samples, printed on coated or uncoated papers, provide tangible evidence of ideas that have already been used successfully. The sample department of a local paper merchant is a good source of supply for this type of material.

Paper Mill Visits

Another excellent way to gain familiarity with paper is to visit paper mills, both those manufacturing coated and uncoated paper. Not only will you gain a better appreciation for the art of paper making but you will also see the various quality-control steps in producing papers on the market today (see figures 11–8 and 11–9).

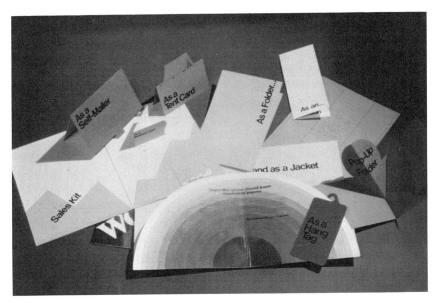

Figures 11-8 and 11-9. Formal demonstrations of printability are available from paper mills through their local paper-merchant distributors. These demonstrations can help with the final selection of paper.

Figure 11-10. Many paper mills and merchants maintain their own idea centers where commercial printing samples are available to show how paper has been used successfully for other applications.

Trade Shows and Seminars

Attendance at trade shows featuring paper manufacturers and paper merchants is another way of gaining additional information about the availability of paper, as are seminars specializing in paper. In addition, paper merchants often conduct open houses or mini–trade shows, to which they invite representatives of paper mills and exhibit their companies' particular types of paper (see figure 11–10).

Modern paper-making and printing technology have improved both the manufacturing of papers and the processes used to print on them, so that you can be fairly certain that your choice will work on the printing press. Whether you select a bold color, a distinctive texture, or the smoothest coated paper surface, there is reason to be confident about printability. How well paper works to make an impact on your printed piece is largely up to you. Remember: your paper selection does have the power to make a difference.

Paul A. Malchow

Managing 12 Printing Projects

In today's world of technological specialization, the production manager must combine time-honored management skills with his or her knowledge of the changing reproduction processes. The successful manager understands the creative working relationship between the copywriter, designer, typesetter, and printer, coordinating the efforts of each to produce an attractive printed piece, on schedule and at a moderate cost.

Coordinating the Elements of a Project

In any printed piece there are four basic human creative elements involved, from the time of inception through completion: conceiver, designer (artist), typesetter, and manufacturer (printer). The writer, editor, or client will frequently be key in preliminary planning. The designer is responsible for taking the idea, words, and art and placing them in an order that is pleasing and attractive to the viewer. The typesetter uses the designer's specifications to create an exact mechanical or reproduction of the designer's idea, with the type and art in place. The manufacturer, using these mechanicals in conjunction with the production specifications, will print reproductions on some media material and finish the package. (Typesetting, design, preparation of graphic materials, and the various printing processes are covered in other chapters; refer to the Table of Contents.)

143

The Project Manager

The project manager oversees each of these contributors and coordinates their contributions with the production schedule. The limitless variety of printed products available in the world today necessitates an early interaction, through the project manager, between the conceiver and the manufacturer. The project manager should avail him or herself to the conceiver and designer when the initial decisions about the project are made. This will help to ensure that the project being worked upon by a staff member or freelancer is capable of being manufactured using the methods planned, at a reasonable cost. This will also enable aesthetic disagreements between design staff members and writers, editors, and so on to be worked out far in advance of production.

Scheduling

Scheduling can be a painstakingly difficult task, but it is critical to a good project manager's repertoire of skills. Frequently it seems as if people want to know when a job is going to be finished even before work has begun.

Scheduling is usually done backwards. The scheduler (project manager) has a deadline from which to derive the date when mechanicals must be shipped to the printer, the date mechanicals must be approved by the art and design staff, the date typesetting and art photography must begin, and so on.

The single most important factor to remember in preparing production schedules is that the time-frames must be accurate. Errors in time-frames will have a snowball effect on the remaining tasks in the schedule.

When preparing a preproduction schedule, make sure the information is accurate. Do not hesitate to contact your printer in the early stages of planning a project. Again, if a step early in the production process is not completed on schedule, it will adversely affect the remaining scheduled steps. Many of the more specialized job shops—design studios, color separation houses, and so on—schedule their work very carefully, some so far as to alter the number of employees on staff to correspond with planned work loads. Therefore, if you do not make your scheduled date to the printer, you may not receive the same turnaround time for that stage as originally planned.

The same rule is true of smaller commercial print shops, though they are not as likely to change the number of employees on hand at any given time.

It is usually wise to contact the typesetter, art studio, and printer before scheduling any job. Discuss with each the project's specifications, cost guidelines, and schedule requirements. The shop managers, customer service representatives, and sales staff are experienced professionals and can be of great help in solving difficult production problems.

Ultimately, the amount of time required to complete any phase of the project is dependent upon three factors: (1) the shop's workload; (2) size of the job (number of pages, copies); and (3) the complexity of the job. Rest assured that no matter how difficult the problem seems, somebody has undoubtedly experienced a similar one before.

A Sample Case

Let's assume you are involved in producing a 16-page advertising piece for the Acme Trailer Corp. The first thing to do is contact the person who brought in the business. Find out exactly what kind of project you are dealing with; after all, "a 16-page piece" does not tell you very much about production or design specification.

A few sample questions you will want to ask:

- What trim size is the piece to be?
- What kind of print material (paper, other) is to be used?
- How many colors will the piece be printed in?
- How many copies of the finished product are required?
- What is the artwork plan?
- How will the project be packaged after printing?
- When are the finished products needed?
- What is the project's estimated budget?

Armed with this preliminary information, you can begin creating a production plan, schedule, and budget. Let us assume that this project, entitled "A Guide to Winterizing Your Trailer," will be 16 pages long, printed on glossy white paper in two colors, 8½ by 11 inches in finished size, and covered with a heavy paper stock printed in four colors. Four thousand finished booklets must be delivered in five months and should have an investment budget of $6,000 in goods and services. This includes everything from designing the piece through shipping the final products.

After learning the project specifications, determine whether or not anything about the project requires you to solicit cost estimates from outside suppliers before beginning production. Among the factors that must be considered are number of colors, artwork involved, unusual typographic demands, number of final products required (print–run size), unusual type or size of finished product, or a schedule so tight it may require special planning or budgeting.

Of course, if the type of product is completely new to you, you will have to solicit cost and schedule estimates for everything. The word *unusual* here refers only to the project manager's past experience. If you are a newcomer to the field or trying to manage your own project for the first time, you may have to request cost and/or schedule estimates for all phases of the project. More experienced managers pick from past experience to plan and budget many projects.

With this information in hand you can proceed to plan, schedule, and budget the project.

Planning

The copy of the guide will be delivered as a typewritten manuscript, with rough outlines of the artwork. Therefore, the first production step will involve evaluating the copy, designing it, and preparing the copy for execution. Before receiving the copy and illustration roughs, write to or telephone a few printers appropriate for the job and review with them your project's specifications and schedule requirements. Request from each a cost estimate and an estimate of the project's completion time (see figure 12–1).

You will find it easier to evaluate each estimate if all are in the same measure, so request that suppliers submit costs in unit terms. The printing and finishing costs fit a learning curve quite nicely, so most project managers request cost estimates for quantities both above and below the expected first-printing quantity. (An explanation of the learning curve and its role in estimating production costs is beyond the scope of this work; I refer readers to *Estimating Manufacturing Costs,* by Lawrence Matthews; McGraw-Hill, 1982.)

You may also want to request cost estimates from typesetters, since a $6,000 budget does not leave much room for error (see figure 12–2). Request estimates in total cost for a small job such as this; for

Mr. Joseph Appleton
Big Apple Printing Co.
123 Orchard Way
Evanston, IL 03054

Dear Joe:

I will be purchasing the printing and binding of an 8½ x 11 inch,
16-page, two-color booklet during May of this year.
Given the specifications below, please provide me with an
estimated unit cost and an estimated production time schedule for
each of the quantities listed.

TRIM: 8½ x 11 inches
COLORS: PMS 181, black
MATERIAL: mechanicals provided
PAPER: you supply, 40# uncoated
COVER: printed two sides, four colors, on 70# coated stock
SCHEDULE: mechanicals to you 1st week May; finished project
                to ship 4th week May
BINDING: saddle-stitched (staples)
QUANTITY: 2,000, 3,000, 4,000, 5,000
PROOFS: books blues before on press

Thank you for your prompt attention to this matter. If you
require any further information, please don't hesitate to call.

Sincerely yours,

Figure 12-1. A typical letter requesting a cost estimate from a printer.

larger, more complex typesetting projects, it is wise to ask for estimates
of each element.

Evaluating copy and rough illustrations is a production-planning
step during which many potential problems are discovered and corrected *before* the project gets into a real-time production mode. For
instance, an alert project manager may notice at this time any copy
that is incorrect in length (this is determined by copy-fitting, discussed
in chapter 9); rough illustration drafts that are not clear enough in
objective for a draftsperson or artist to execute; or halftones (or photographs) that are not of acceptable graphic quality. This initial eval-
uation is not the project manager's task alone; it is very important

Ms. Marilyn Mabage
Patch Typesetters Inc.
1223 N. Main St.
Evanston, IL 03452

Dear Marilyn:

I would like a typesetting estimate based on the enclosed
duplicate copy and the following specifications:

NUMBER OF TYPESET PAGES: 16
NUMBER OF COLORS: 2 colors
NUMBER OF LINE   8
  ILLUSTRATIONS:
NUMBER OF HALFTONES: 3
PROOF TYPE, NUMBER   pages, 3 sets; positive
  OF SETS: mechanicals,
   1 set
SHIP TO YOU: 1st week April
SHIP PAGE PROOF: 3rd week April
SHIP MECHANICALS: 4th week April

I plan to hold the page proofs for only three days. If you need any
further information, please don't hesitate to call. Thank you.

Sincerely yours,

Figure 12-2. A typical letter requesting a cost estimate from a typesetter.

that the project's art director, designer, and copywriter or copy editor
review the material as well.

Once the cost estimates have been received from potential printers
and typesetters, the project manager must evaluate them and make
a decision. The final selection should be based on at least three basic
measures: (1) the price supplied by the potential vendor; (2) the
schedule approved by the supplier; and (3) the supplier's past performance in meeting price/schedule commitments.

The job-assignment decision criteria are always dependent upon
the project manager's focus on the project. In cases in which the
project's schedule is critical, some sacrifices may be made concerning
the price paid for the service. Because of this, the most attractive

cost estimate should not necessarily assure that the job will be awarded to that company.

Another very important aspect of preliminary project planning is the ordering of materials. Most printers stock many of the most commonly used print media (paper) and will be more than happy to supply the material to you. But for jobs calling for some unusual material, you may need to order what is required and have it delivered to the printer. Usually this ordering is done through a paper distributing company, but if the material is very uncommon or needed in large quantities, it may be more advantageous to order directly from the manufacturer.

The trade-off here is that while you are likely to receive a better price by going directly to the manufacturer (providing the quantity is large enough), the order time (the time from order to delivery) is likely to be greater, and smaller companies may have to pay in advance for at least part of the order. For this reason it is usually preferable for the small company to buy the materials from the printer when possible or from a distributor if not.

This factor may also affect your decision about printing assignments. A printer who stocks the necessary material may be preferred to his competitor, even if the competitor has submitted a more attractive bid for the project. Manufacturers and distributors will have timetables for delivery of special-order materials. Thus, if you are using special materials in a printed project, make contact with the supplier regarding material availability and delivery schedules early in the preproduction planning stage.

Once the suppliers have been chosen, the schedule and budget established, and the copy approved, the project can proceed to the design and editing stage.

Managing Design and Editing

Design and editing, unlike other aspects of graphic-project management, are usually tasks performed by individual craftspeople. The management of this phase of the production process tends to require more of a hands-off style than that of the other portions of the production process. It may be best to establish a budget and schedule let these people do their jobs. (For more on design, see chapters 8, 9, and 10; for more on editing and proofreading, see chapter 13.)

Scheduling of Printing Projects

No matter what special considerations your chosen printing process may require (as previous chapters devoted to various printing processes have indicated), the scheduling of your project will always break down into four major steps: (1) preparation of copy; (2) checking proofs before the job goes to press; (3) the press run or actual time the job will be on press; and (4) finishing operations such as binding, die-cutting, or other special treatment.

The scheduling question of sheet-fed versus roll or web printing is one that is usually governed by the size of the press run. As a rule of thumb, web presses are favored over sheet-fed for long (large-quantity) press runs.

Press-run time is directly proportional to the number of units being produced and is often referred to as impressions per hour, or feet per minute for web presses. This is where the learning curve comes into play. The actual printing of an item is the least labor-intensive of all of the processes leading to a printed piece. Thus, the longer the project stays on press or the greater the number of pieces produced, the lower the cost for each piece will be. This is true for all types of printing, so your printer's salespeople should be able to supply figures to help you estimate run time.

Scheduling the finishing of printed projects is difficult because of the many different types of finishing techniques available (see chapter 14). Finishing covers everything from a stapled (saddle stitched) pamphlet to a die-cut booklet. The large number of variables makes it imperative to establish the finishing time with the finisher in pre-production planning, unless you have had previous experience with the type of finishing under consideration.

A warning here: always make sure you have anticipated the constraints the finishing procedure may place upon your project. These constraints will show up in preliminary planning, budgeting, mechanical production, and printing. For example, certain types of glue binding require that the printed sheets have about ⅛ inch shaved off the binding side before glue is placed. In this case, the designer of the project should specify ample room in the margin to allow for this, to avoid losing any part of the printed material. If your finishing method requires any complex die-cutting, folding, or trimming, make sure you receive finishing proofs before the mechanicals are prepared for printing.

This brings up an important distinction in types of proofs. Often, printers will ask if you want confirming proofs as opposed to regular proofs. The difference is critical: confirming proofs do not always offer a chance to correct any errors found; they are provided as a last check before you see the finished product, with changes made only in the case of an absolute disaster. Never accept confirming proofs as your only checking point unless you have 100 percent confidence in the product, and even then, you should think twice.

Product Packaging and Finishing Methods

Although it is beyond the scope of this book to explore all the ways of packaging or finishing a printed product, we have one word of advice: if faced with an unusual or unknown finishing procedure, *do not try to bluff your way through it.*

Finishing usually involves precise measurement, bonding, and alignment of many unseen seams, joints, and corners. Consult with your supplier's representative before beginning artwork or mechanical production for the binding or finishing portion of the project. If you do not know a supplier capable of producing the needed type of finishing, check with other printing plants or with Printing Industries of America, a trade association located in Arlington, Virginia.

Always request a binding/finishing proof for approval before the project proceeds to the finishing area. The finished package, cover, case, or binding is often the first and sometimes only part a consumer looks at. Its importance must not be underestimated.

A Planning Checklist

Doing the following will help your printing project go smoothly:
• Have a fairly clear idea of the job's purpose, how it will be presented, and in what form (hardcover book, pamphlet, catalog).
• Plan for the distribution of the finished piece (when, where, by whom) and the estimated press run.

• Determine the number of colors to be printed and the type of material the piece will be printed on.

• Estimate the entire budget, including printing, outside suppliers, and finishing, if necessary.

• Choose the type of printing press appropriate for the job and within your budget.

• Map out a production schedule, coordinated with each step along the way (editing, typesetting, design, mechanicals, proofs, printing, binding, delivery/distribution).

• When in doubt, or if you have a question or problem, check immediately with the person(s) involved. Under any circumstances, keep in touch with those with whom you are working on the project.

Editing 13
and Proofreading

Editing and proofreading are vital steps in the printing process. Without them the good will of the reading public would be sorely tested.

Editing can be loosely defined as the preparation of a manuscript or piece of copy for publication. Two distinct editing functions fall under this general term: (1) substantive or line editing and (2) copy-editing. The first function includes analyzing a manuscript's organization, rewriting or suggesting that the author rewrite passages of the work, and querying the author when material is unclear, incorrect, or missing.

Copy-editing is the more technical task of imposing a standard form for spelling and punctuation, improving and correcting grammar and syntax, spot-checking facts, and, in some cases, marking the manuscript for the designer. The copy editor gives a manuscript its final polishing before it goes to the typesetter (see chapter 9).

Proofreading is the reading of one version of a work against another in order to catch errors. This usually means reading typeset galley proofs against the original manuscript and later reading page proofs or reproduction copy against the galleys.

Ideally, each function is performed by a different person. Three heads are certainly better than one or two when it comes to catching errors in copy. This ideal is not always practical, however, and one person may have to take on all three tasks. If any consolidating is necessary, it is preferable that one person cover the editing functions and another the proofreading. It becomes easier to miss errors when a work is overly familiar.

The following discussion should be general enough to apply to functions of preparing copy for any type of printing job, despite the obvious differences one can expect from project to project. Be advised, too, that much of the following applies to editing and proofreading that are performed in a traditional, manual manner. The advent of electronic word processing and text editing has sometimes changed these functions, so that much editing can now be performed on a word processor's CRT screen, sidestepping many of the manual procedures. Moreover, coordination between author and editor can be accomplished via networked electronic equipment, or else an author might simply deliver a memory disk containing a manuscript to the editor. (For more information on word processing, refer to chapter 16.)

Substantive Editing

A substantive editor is the best friend an author can have. This worthy soul frequently encourages an author when an impasse is reached on a writing project, suggests a focus when the amount of information seems overwhelming, and helps develop a framework for the opus. But the true value of an editor is usually seen after a manuscript's completion. Pencil in hand, the editor analyzes every word for sense and accuracy, untangles convoluted passages, suggests remedies for weak areas, and queries the author whenever a point is unclear or information is missing. This behind-the-scenes work enhances the reputation of the author, whose written work is put in the best possible light.

To be most effective, an editor should possess two key qualities: (1) comprehensiveness, in order to judge how well the parts of a written work fit together, and (2) acuteness, in order to recognize which words and sentences need emending. The ability to write logically and clearly is essential, as is facility with language. An editor also needs an endless supply of tact. Most writers are highly sensitive, so diplomacy in phrasing questions and suggesting changes to them is essential. Sarcasm and condescension are both unprofessional and inefficient means of soliciting cooperation from a writer. What is more, extensive editing without the author's approval may sometimes create legal problems.

Preliminary Guidelines for the Author

Before the author types the final manuscript, make sure you have communicated what your preferred format is. Editors normally require that manuscripts be typed on white nonerasable bond measuring 8½ by 11 inches. All copy, including extracts, lists, and footnotes, should be double-spaced, leaving a minimum of one-inch margins on both sides of every page to allow room for editing marks and emendations. Pica type is usually preferred over elite, although either is acceptable. Whichever size is chosen should be used throughout in consideration of the designer charged with estimating the length of the printed work (this "copy-fitting" function is explained in chapter 9).

The author should number all text pages consecutively. If at any point a page is deleted or inserted in a numbered manuscript, this should be noted beside the numbers on the preceding and following pages. If an insertion does not fill a full page, a line should be drawn to the bottom of the page to show that more copy follows.

Tables and illustrations should not be numbered with the manuscript. Instead, each should bear the table or figure number it will carry in the printed work. This number should be keyed to the text by writing it in the margin of the text it will accompany. If illustrations, perhaps photographs, will not be numbered in the final form, they can be assigned consecutive numbers for keying.

First Reading

Unless you are already familiar with a manuscript, you will probably want to read it through after its arrival. Keep a pen and a pad of paper handy to jot down notes as you read. The most important thing to determine at this point is whether or not the material is acceptable for publication. This can be a subjective decision; usually, however, a manuscript has to be very poor to be deemed unacceptable, such as if it is incomplete, poorly researched, or sloppily written and organized, or if it concerns a topic other than the one agreed upon in the publishing contract.

Fortunately, most manuscripts are acceptable as submitted. This is not to say they are free of major problems. If a manuscript is poorly written, the author may be able to improve it with editorial guidance. If, in your judgment, the author is incapable of rewriting the manuscript, you may want to call in a rewriter. In some cases you may decide to rewrite portions of a work yourself. Do not undertake this task, however, without carefully considering the time and effort involved; rewriting could take you from other editing projects.

The next thing to determine in your initial reading is how well the manuscript is structured. If you are working on a book, do the chapters fall in the most logical order? If you are editing a shorter piece, is it developed in a direct, understandable manner? If the material is instructional, are the directions given sequentially? Does the text move from the easiest to the most difficult projects? If the matter is historical, is chronology respected? If it is advertising copy, does it succinctly get to the point of selling the product or service?

During the first reading, also make a point of checking that the author has made no major omissions, and note any weak areas or recurring problems. After this initial read-through you may want to shuffle any major portions of out-of-sequence material. Confer with the author before jumping in, however; there may have been a particular purpose to the present arrangement, and after your discussion you may see another approach to restructuring the material. Even if you do proceed with your original plan for reorganization, do so with the author's approval. Do not spend time analyzing the placement of every sentence and paragraph at this point. Shorter portions of the work are more easily transposed during the line editing.

Blue Penciling

Now that you can see where you are heading, you are ready to begin. Because the typesetter will follow the copy as he or she sets type, make all editorial marks and additions directly in the copy or as close to where they belong as possible. Several marks are useful in emending copy; see figure 13-1 for a listing of proofreaders' symbols. Make all your marks as clearly as possible for the typesetter. If the author adds anything that is hard to read, recopy it or have it retyped.

The author can be queried in the margins, on slips of paper (flags) glued to the back of a manuscript page at the right-hand edge and folded to the front, or on separate pages. Many editors prefer flags because they are easy to use and can be removed before the manuscript

Instruction	Notation in margin	Notation in type	Corrected type
Delete		the ~~type~~ font	the font
Insert	type	the font	the type font
Let it stand	stet	the type font	the type font
Reset in capitals	cap	the type font	THE TYPE FONT
Reset in lowercase	lc	THE TYPE FONT	the type font
Reset in italics	ital	the type font	the *type* font
Reset in small capitals	sc	See type font	See TYPE FONT
Reset in roman	rom	the *type* font	the type font
Reset in boldface	bf	the type font	**the type font**
Reset in lightface	lf	the type font	the type font
Transpose	tr	the font type	the type font
Close up space		the ty pe	the type
Delete and close space		the type foont	the type font
Move left		the type font	the type font
Move right		the type font	the type font
Run in	run in	The type font is Univers. It is not Garamond.	The type font is Univers. It is not Garamond.
Align		the type font the type font the type font	the type font the type font the type font
Spell out	sp	3 type fonts	Three type fonts
Insert space	#	the type font	the type font
Insert period		The type font	The type font.
Insert comma		One two, three	One, two, three
Insert hyphen		Ten point type	Ten-point type

Figure 13-1. Proofreaders' symbols.

Instruction	Notation in margin	Notation in type	Corrected type
Insert colon	(:)	Old Style types	Old Style types:
Insert semicolon	;	Select the font spec the type.	Select the font; spec the type.
Insert apostrophe	'	Baskervilles type	Baskerville's type
Insert quotation marks	"/"/	the word type	the word "type"
Insert parenthesis	(/)/	The word type is in parenthesis.	The word (type) is in parenthesis.
Insert en dash	1/N	Flush left	Flush-left
Insert em dash	1/M/ 1/M/	Garamond an Old Style face is used today.	Garamond — an Old Style face — is used today.
Start paragraph	¶	The type font is Univers 55.	The type font is Univers 55.
No paragraph indent	no ¶	The type font is Univers 55.	The type font is Univers 55.

Figure 13-1, continued.

goes to the typesetter. Queries written in the margins should be erased before typesetting.

If you write in the margins or on flags, ask the author not to erase your remarks or remove the flags, since they are the only record of your queries. You will need them to locate the author's responses.

Many colors of pencil may be used in editing: plain lead, green, red, purple, and brown are as acceptable as the traditional blue, and they may even be preferable if you plan to photocopy the edited manuscript, since blue pencil is often difficult to reproduce photographically. Whatever color you choose, stick with it. The author, editor, copy editor, and designer should each have his or her distinctive color.

Some Guidelines for the Editor

While much in editing depends on the editor's judgment and discernment, certain general guidelines do apply. Keep the following steps in mind as you tackle a nonfiction manuscript. (Editing fiction is a specialty that requires attention to such things as the logical progression of the plot and the believability of the characters' actions.)

1. Analyze the organization. As already mentioned, you might need to rearrange misplaced material as you edit. Make sure your intentions are clear to the typesetter. You may find it necessary to cut apart the manuscript and paste or tape the copy in its new order. To ensure that each new page measures 8½ by 11 inches, tape the pieces of copy to a clean sheet of white paper.

2. Study the headlines, both primary and secondary or subheadings. Are they too long? Do they accurately reflect the copy they precede? Are there enough of them? Are there too many? Be sure that all heads and subheads are clear and correctly placed.

3. Generally speaking, never tamper with the writing style. If the only thing wrong with a sentence is that you do not care for it, leave it alone. If you can objectively state a reason for the need to rewrite a passage, you are justified in altering it.

4. Check for sense. A sentence may sound beautiful but mean nothing. If the author leaves gaps, is unclear or contradictory, or in other ways fails to convey a message, query the author on the meaning and suggest how the passage might be improved.

5. Observe standard rules of grammar. Occasionally an infraction of the rules is highly effective and should be left alone. But if nothing is gained by a disagreement of verb and subject, faulty attempts at parallel construction, or other grammatical errors, rephrase the copy to conform to the rules.

6. Watch for redundancies. Some repetition of ideas may be necessary for reinforcement, but mentioning the same point more than a few times is tedious for the reader and suggests that the writer does not have much to say. Also be alert to overuse of clichés and pet words and phrases; ask the author to supply substitutes where necessary and delete those that add nothing to the text.

7. Delete extraneous material. Anything that does not add to the meaning or effect of the work should be taken out.

8. Check for completeness. Is something missing? Has the author satisfactorily explained his or her ideas? If not, point out which areas need amplifying.

9. Is the information accurate? Supplying correct references and factual material is the author's responsibility, but be on your toes to catch anything that sounds odd, and query the author about it. You

would know that something is awry, for instance, in a cookie recipe calling for three tablespoons of salt.

10. Are claims substantiated? Even in a piece that is mainly opinion, the writer should be able to support stands that have been taken. Flat statements are not likely to convince anyone, so be sure the author supplies solid evidence or examples to back up any extravagant assertions.

11. Edit for bias. Without meaning to, an author may offend some readers. Any terms or ideas that indicate bias against women, blacks, Hispanics, the elderly, or any other groups should be reworded. Such passages can often be subtle. For example, a sports article referring to men by their last names and to women by their first names may be offensive to women readers. Some publishers have explicit guidelines for treatment of such material.

12. Has the author obtained all the necessary permissions? If more than a few lines are quoted from another work, whether published or not, it is the author's responsibility to secure permission to use the material.

13. Watch for libelous statements. In some manuscripts, notably biographies, an author may make statements that could be construed as libelous. Both author and editor should be alert to check such passages with a lawyer. In advertising copy, certain claims made about a product or service may conflict with ethical standards or specific rules established by the Federal Trade Commission or other regulatory bodies.

14. Prepare the front matter. Before turning over the manuscript to the copy editor, the editor may be required to prepare a half-title page (title only, no subtitle); a title page (title and subtitle, author's name, publisher, and place of publication); copyright page (the publisher should supply the necessary information); and table of contents.

Copy-editing

As usually defined, copy-editing is related to but distinct from substantive editing. It is the final polishing and fine tuning of an author's work. The task can range from simply marking the manuscript for the designer to rewriting paragraphs. A fine line sometimes separates substantive editing from copy-editing. When an editor corrects spelling and punctuation, the process could be labeled copy editing; when a copy editor rewrites passages, the process could be labeled substantive editing. The scope of the copy editor's work may be defined by how much work the line editor devoted to the project. Even so, it should be made clear to a copy editor when a project is assigned exactly how detailed a job is expected.

A copy editor needs patience and an ability to deal carefully and attentively with detailed work. His or her attention should not wander, nor should the copy editor move through the manuscript more quickly than is warranted by the material. Especially important is an aptitude for consistent, thorough work.

In general, a copy editor is concerned with styling the manuscript; correcting spelling and typographical errors; noting obvious factual errors; correcting grammar and syntax; correcting errors of punctuation; marking the manuscript for the designer.

Practical Advice on Style and Usage

Webster's New Collegiate Dictionary defines style as "the custom or plan followed in spelling, capitalization, punctuation, and typographic arrangement and display." Many companies adopt a house style; if your company has no styling preferences, you can develop a style for each manuscript or adhere to certain guidelines on all the manuscripts you copy-edit. The style chosen should be based on a major style book, such as *A Manual of Style,* published by the University of Chicago Press.

Among the considerations in styling a manuscript will be whether or not to use a comma before *and* or *or* in a series; which words to hyphenate; which spelling to use when more than one form is acceptable; whether or not to use an initial cap in a full sentence that follows a colon; how to treat abbreviations; whether to spell out numbers or represent them by figures.

A style sheet is useful in keeping track of such styling decisions. A simple style sheet can be made by dividing several sheets of paper into rectangles, as illustrated in figure 13–2. In each rectangle, enter one, two, or more letters of the alphabet, depending on how many entries you think will fall under each letter. At the end of the alphabet, leave room for decisions reached about the treatment of numbers and other elements. Then simply record your decisions as you make them. It is helpful to jot down the page number beside each entry in case you want to make styling changes later on.

A	B	C
acidic [not acid] (adj) acid solution (double noun) alanine altaite [p.16] Arrhenius aluminosilicate arseniuretted andesite asparagine anion aspartic acid anode austenite aqueous aqua regia aqua fortis alkalie [noun] arginine alkaline [adj] argol arsenides arsenopyrite	Bakelite Balball-Thom cell barite basic [adj] bater [p.27] bauxite beryl bismuthinite "blick" borosilicate Brinell hardness breccia Buchner funnel bullion burette Bunsen burner by-product	calaverite copperas calcareous cornet carnotite corundum carboxylic cryolite Carborundum cupel (ed) [verb] cassiterite cupellation catalyst cupperite [p.14] celestite cyanogen cementite cysteine chelate cystine chloral chrysotile cinnabar clayey [adj] concentrator
D dacite [p.17] decrepitation didymium dimethylglyoxime diorite dioxime [p.80] dilute [not diluted] (adj) dissociated doré bar	**E** electroplating electrorefining electrowinning electrolyte electrolytic cell elutriator encapsulated end product Erlenmeyer flask	**F** feldspar filtrate fluorspar fluosilicate flotation fritting fusible
G galena gangue glutamic acid glycine glyoxime Glauber's salt gneiss greenockite gyratory	**H** hematite heasite histidine hornblende hydrazine hydrofluoric acid hydrochloric acid hydrate hygroscopic hypochlorite	**I** immiscible impure [not unpure] inquartation iridescent isoleucine

Figure 13-2. Sample of an editor's style sheet.

An alternate style sheet can be made by simply arranging elements by the type of decision they embody, as in listing all spelling decisions in one column, all hyphenation decisions in another, and so on.

The style sheet serves more than just the copy editor. The proofreader will also find it useful, as will anyone involved with subsequent editions of the printed piece. The style sheet also shows the author that a plan was followed and that changes were not made randomly.

Quickly reviewing the manuscript at the outset will reveal the major areas of concern. The author may be a poor speller, or the work may be full of historical events, names, and dates. A scientific work full of numbers will require different treatment from an essay on art with only occasional reference to numbers.

The copy editor, like the line editor, should bear in mind that generally speaking, the author's writing style is not to be tampered with. Do correct errors, however, including errors of fact. If much of the text contains dates, names, quantities, and other factual material, one cannot be expected to check every fact unless fact-checking is something that has been specifically assigned. The author is ultimately responsible for the accuracy of the material. If there are queries, keep them brief and pertinent—and tactful.

The copy editor should also note any page references in the text by writing "page ref." or something similar in the margin and circling the note. This will help the author or editor place the correct page number in the text after page proofs or mechanicals have been prepared. Until the correct page numbers, or folios, can be inserted, ciphers should be used to hold the places the numbers will fill. If it is likely that a page reference will refer to a later section of the book, "page 000" can be used; if it will refer to an earlier section, "page 00" will be sufficient. Setting ciphers in boldface (**000**) allows you to find them more easily in galleys.

Cross references should be checked carefully. For instance, if the author refers to a table on cloud types in chapter 2, be sure that the table is there.

Marking the Manuscript

The copy editor may be required to mark for the designer all material that deviates from straight text. This can be done by simply labeling each element with an appropriate abbreviation and then writing a key for your abbreviations. Although you can devise your own abbreviations, the following are frequently used:

   Part number

   Part title

   Chapter number

(CT)   Chapter title

(AN)   Appendix number

(AT)   Appendix title

(1)(2)(3)
(A)(B)(C)   Primary, secondary, and tertiary subheadings

The following marks can be used to identify material for the designer when you also run a vertical rule in the margin to the left of the material.

(EPI)   Epigraph

(NL)   Numbered list

(UNL)   Unnumbered list

(EXT)   Extract

(FN)   Footnote

Proofreading

Proofreading is related to but distinct from editing and copy-editing. It involves catching errors by reading one copy of a work against another. This usually means first checking the galley proofs against the original manuscript and later checking page proofs or reproduction copy against the galleys. In each case, errors and omissions must be marked and corrections made in the clearest possible manner. The proofreader's marks and corrections are generally made in the side margins, because typeset copy is usually more closely spaced than is manuscript copy, and because a typesetter, who revises only those sections marked, needs the corrections to be highly visible.

In addition to correcting errors in the copy, a proofreader should check the appearance of the typeset copy. Was the design followed? Are the lines straight? Are the pages clean? Are any of the characters broken? Have words at the ends of lines been divided correctly? Have any widows been created? (A widow is a fragment of a word sitting alone on a line at the end of a paragraph, or a fragment of a sentence at the end of a paragraph sitting alone at the top of a page. Both should be avoided.)

Proofreading requires attentiveness and meticulousness. Never hurry through a proofreading job; you are sure to miss errors if you do.

Standard practice calls for initialing and dating each page at the bottom right-hand corner after it has been proofread. This prevents unnecessarily rereading material and identifies the reader should questions arise. (Refer again to figure 13-1 for a listing of standard proofreaders' marks.)

Reference Books

Certain reference books are essential to both substantive and copy editors. A good style manual is a must. The University of Chicago Press's *A Manual of Style* (13th edition, 1982) is a favorite among book editors. So is *Words into Type,* by M. Skillin and R. Gay (Prentice-Hall, 1974). For styling magazine and newspaper articles, you might refer to *The New York Times Manual of Style and Usage,* by Lewis Jordan (Times Books, 1976).

A good book on grammar and usage is another necessity. William Strunk and E. B. White's *Elements of Style* (Macmillan, 1978) is a slim classic. Also recommended are Henry W. Fowler's *Dictionary of Modern English Usage* (Oxford University Press, 1965); *The Complete Stylist and Handbook,* by Sheridan Baker (2nd edition, Harper & Row, 1980); *Macmillan Handbook of English,* by John M. Kierzek and Walter Gibson (6th edition, Macmillan, 1977); and *The Careful Writer: A Modern Guide to English Usage,* by Theodore M. Bernstein (Atheneum, 1965).

Ideally, an editor should own two or more dictionaries. *Webster's Third New International Dictionary, Unabridged* (Merriam, 1976) is a good choice. The *Random House Dictionary of the English Language* (Random House, 1966) is helpful for the language dictionaries it includes at the back. Check with your publisher to see which dictionary is preferred.

Other basic reference books include a biographical dictionary (the Webster's published by Merriam is recommended); John Bartlett's

Familiar Quotations (Little, Brown, 1980); a thesaurus (*Roget's International Thesaurus,* published by T. Y. Crowell, is usually considered the best); the latest world almanac; an atlas; and a King James version of the Bible. A one-volume encyclopedia might also prove useful, as will technical and English/foreign language dictionaries.

A proofreader needs at the least an unabridged dictionary and a small book of word divisions (based on a dictionary approved by the publisher), as well as a style manual.

Of interest to both editors and proofreaders is *Bookmaking: The Illustrated Guide to Design/Production/Editing,* by Marshall Lee (Bowker, 1980).

The Bindery: 14
Folding, Die-Cutting, and Finishing

To a printer, the bindery is where it all comes together. Because of the many tasks performed in this segment of graphic arts, and because of the seeming confusion created by the furor of work in the bindery, it has been labeled by some as "that great swamp." In today's pattern of work-flow, where the tendency is to perform different printing and assembly duties in separate plants, not all printers maintain a bindery as part of their operation. Some prefer to contract for binding outside their own facilities, usually at an independent shop. But because there are not as many such binderies today as there were a few years ago, the printer must provide at least some degree of bindery service for his customers.

The Bindery

Periodical publishers tend to place their work with "full-service" printers, where at least the collating, stitching, and trimming of their publications are done "on-line," or as part of a continuous work-flow, following presswork, within the confines of one plant. Publishers hope this setup will expedite the shipment of their publications, cut spoilage, and maintain better security for their product. For conventional commercial printing of posters, brochures, labels, and other similar work, the printer may install limited cutting, folding, or specialized equipment designed to handle, in-house, the majority of the work attached to the production of a customer's job.

A complete bindery serves the needs of many diversified clients and must be equipped with a wide variety of machinery, which may often remain idle between specialized jobs. Further, a bindery requires a sizable staff to perform a large number of hand operations not ideally suited for machines. This is particularly true of shops that are called upon to handle short print-runs, specialty gluing, hand folding, mounting, and finishing operations.

While commercial printing might be considered the bread and butter of the industry, folding, die-cutting, and finishing are the frosting on the cake. *Folding* is a common enough term, so it needs little explanation here other than to define the various folds available both on press (particularly on high-speed, publication presses) and the off-machine folds. The latter are more typical of commercial work and involve simple, short-run booklets, forms, and individual sheets, or more complex press signatures, maps, parallel, right-angle, or accordion folds. These will all be dealt with later in this chapter.

Die-cutting is a fanciful art, very much in vogue for attractive, compelling, point-of-purchase (p-o-p) cards; odd-shaped labels; greeting cards; more complex window posters; or pop-up promotion pieces (see chapter 1). This specialty craft adds elegance and creative style to commemorative pieces, animated cutouts, trick-fold calendars, and an almost limitless variety of designs fancied by an imaginative art director. This interesting technique, too, will be discussed in full.

The term *finishing* encompasses a wide range of services, generally following presswork, often considered part of the bindery operation but broadened in scope to include a number of specialty services including folding and die-cutting mentioned above. Falling in this category are such refinements as laminating, bronzing, drilling or punching, padding, foil stamping, cutting, creasing, embossing, gluing, tipping, and so on. Finishing is all that the word implies: the completion and enhancement of a product to give it the final touch, which in turn will attract the reader, the buyer, or the client.

Some finishing operations are performed on-line, as mentioned earlier, as an adjunct to web-press printing, such as folded signatures delivered from a book, magazine, or newspaper press, sometimes with pages or cards "tipped in" or leaves pasted together. In packaging, the finishing may entail cutting, creasing, scoring, or stripping. For more delicate work, often in small-quantity orders, the finishing might call for a certain amount of handwork for special gluing, folding, or inserting, even though there is hardly a specialty job today for which some piece of machinery has not been devised or altered to do the job mechanically. If a designer can produce an original copy of a flip-top box, an intricate cutout, or a trick fold, the chances are that a good die-cut expert or finisher can find a way of producing multiple copies at high speed on modern equipment now available.

When design is limited to simple forms, such constraint is usually the result of not enough time (too exacting a schedule), a volume too great for complex handwork, or, more frequently, a limited budget. This is not to say that good design cannot be simple in structure. Quite the contrary. Simplicity itself is often a thing of beauty. For instance, foil stampings, with their use of rich metallics, embossings with no printing at all but merely raised design, and interesting, effective die-cuts can make all the difference between an ordinary design and a booklet or commemorative folder that bespeaks richness and charm. Such techniques can help create a true keepsake that the recipient will carry away and cherish as a valuable reminder of any occasion for years to come.

Folding

Folding can be broken down into two categories: (1) on-press folding, usually associated with a high-speed web press, but also with a sheet-fed press; and (2) off-press specialty folding which calls for unique machines capable of producing an infinite variety of tucks and flaps, depending upon the settings of rollers and/or tucker blades that make up the complex workings of the machine.

The basic units that comprise the folder mechanism on a web press include a former, over which the web of paper travels after the printing; a tucker blade; and a series of rollers. The blade tucks the web between the rollers to complete the first fold. Multiple folds are possible depending on the number of rollers and their position in the folder. A knife-blade chopper completes the cycle by separating the folded unit from the rest of the web.

Considering the fact that the modern web press travels at speeds upwards of 2,000 feet per minute, the split-second folding and cutting operation calls for sophisticated machinery to execute the proper fold accurately and to duplicate it thousands of times over in the course of the complete press run. Folders on a web press can be adjusted to handle a variety of folds, delivering units of 4, 8, 16, or 32 pages in a "signature" ready for the bindery. In some instances, such as in a folded unit ready for mailing or inserting in a newspaper as a supplement, it is an important adjunct to a publication press. A large press, capable of printing 64 pages of a magazine at one run-through, may deliver from several trays in smaller units of 32 pages from one tray and two 16s or four 8s from the other trays. Press delivery depends upon the folder settings and how it has been programmed to deliver.

Depending upon the width of the paper roll or web, some folders are capable of producing "gatefolds," commonly seen as magazine covers affording a three-page spread. There is even a four-page "double gate," for maximum four-page spread exposure of an illustration of an advertiser's product. Variations of the gatefold—half-page gates, Dutch doors, French or Venetian doors, and so on—are also possible but are more commonly found in direct-mail pieces, which are generally handled "off press," or by an outside supplier. (For more on direct mail, see chapter 15.)

Other forms of finishing possible on the modern-day webs include on-press perforations, numbering, scoring, or pasting. A press equipped with a paster can deliver a self-contained booklet with folded leaves pasted together at the gutter with no further bindery steps necessary after the booklet is delivered from the press. Such booklets are commonly found inserted in newspapers as television guides or special sales catalogs. For the more sophisticated color magazine supplements, it is possible to equip a press with a wire stitcher head for binding these units together with staples.

Most magazines seen on newsstands are bound off-press and consist of an assortment of different signatures delivered from separate presses, collated and saddle-stitched on an automatic binding machine. In this type of magazine finishing, the publication is trimmed—head, foot, and front—with a three-knife trimmer, which is an on-line attachment to the collator and stitcher. Other types of magazine binding include the popular "square back" or perfect bind, which uses plastic adhesives and replaces the old side-wire bind (staples) popular a number of years ago.

Cutting to Size

The conventional method of folding a flat sheet is accomplished with one of the many off-press folders, designed to be used for almost any purpose a technician dictates. If the press sheet is oversized, it might be necessary to first cut it to a more manageable size, particularly if it was initially printed in multiples as a two-, four-, or eight-form. This type of cutting is generally done on a large guillotine trimmer.

These large machines noted for their power, rugged construction, and accuracy, sometimes have built-in microcomputer controls and interchangeable memories and can be programmed to repeat complex cutting sequences automatically. There are completely automatic work-flow "systems" that can be operated by one person, loading and unloading. The stock to be cut will be taken off the skid pile and transported to the cutter. The cutter clamp opening determines the maximum height of the pile to be selected. Following the cutting operation, the stock is automatically transferred onto pallets in a precise pile. The cutting machine is then unloaded and prepared to accept an incoming load.

Less complex cutting machines call for hand feeding of paper. All feature the latest in safety devices, making it impossible to keep hands or fingers near the cutting blade when they are being operated.

After large sheets have been cut, many folding combinations can be used to create map folds, accordion folds, tuck folds, squares, oblongs, and triangles, limited only by the designer's imagination. As for the machines themselves, there are two basic types, (1) the buckle folder and (2) the tuck or knife folder. On a buckle folder, each section has feeding and folding rollers, one or more hollow plates, and an adjustable stop. Depending upon the folder setting and the combination of rollers, many different folds are possible. The tuck fold is the simpler of the two types. A blade tucks a sheet of paper between two rollers, which in turn forms the fold.

Folders vary in size from some units that can handle sheets of 18 by 25 inches or smaller up to other machines built to handle sheets 72 inches long. These machines can slit large sheets into several sections, as well as fold, and can deliver up to four or more sections at a time. Scoring and perforating can also be performed on properly equipped folders. Slitting wheels with sharp edges are mounted on shafts between the folding sections. As the paper passes through the folder, it is held against the cutting wheel by rollers. For perforating, a serrated-edge wheel is substituted for the slitter wheel. Various combinations of slitting, scoring, perforating, and folding are possible on such a machine.

Die-Cutting

The specialty craft of die-cutting can add elegance and creative styling to almost any printed piece, including booklets, commemorative presentations, p-o-p displays, and other show cards, especially when they are combined with other unusual finishing touches such as foil stamping or embossing. One often sees "windows" cut in greeting cards, pop-up promotions, animated cutouts, or unusual calendars enhanced with "trick" die-cuts. On a larger scale, die-cutting is used for display easels, cardboard cutouts, posters, and heavy cartons. Here again, the concepts are limited only by the designer's art.

There are two primary methods of die-cutting in use today: (1) hollow die-cutting and (2) steel-rule cutting. The former is used mainly for such stock items as envelopes and labels, which do not require internal cutouts, perforations, or scoring. For steel-rule die-cutting, sharp-edged rules can be formed in any design and used much in the manner of a cookie cutter to punch through a thickness of sheets chosen to carry the design.

Most die-cutting is done on flatbed letterpress presses, converted for the purpose, with the inking rollers removed. Rotary die-cutters are also used for such repeat items as milk cartons and specialty packaging.

In the preparation stage for creating a steel-rule die, a sketch of the desired design or cutout is made on a wooden base, usually a piece of ¾-inch plywood. The sketch is traced over with a jigsaw, cutting a slot or groove in the block; into this the steel-rule cutting edges are implanted, with the raised cutting edge exposed at type-high levels. The rules are formed by bending, with machine-shop tools, to fit the slotted pattern. Strips of molded rubber are cemented to the wood block on either side of the blade edge to cushion the impact of the die-cut, making it easier for blade withdrawal after cutting without damage to the paper.

These blocks of wood, with their steel cutting blades, are locked onto the press much in the manner of making-ready a conventional printing press. In the case of die-cutting, the block and cutting edges are substituted for type in a locked-up chase. Depending upon the thickness of the paper or substrate to be cut, the sheets may be fed into the press for cutting one at a time or in multiple thicknesses.

While we think of die-cutting only as it applies to the printing industry, it is a technique used in other industries for cutting machine gaskets, plastics, wood, or metal machine parts as well. In printing, it can serve a utilitarian purpose by cutting slots for inserting cards or other printed matter, as well as providing windows to view through an outer cover or top sheet the copy or design underneath. A sheet of transparent film or acetate is sometimes tipped to the inside of a die-cut or cutout, to provide a true window, either for protection or further enhancement of the design.

The die-cutter's art is an exacting one and if properly executed can add immeasurably to the appearance or the utilization of a p-o-p display, presentation piece, or promotion mailer.

Die-Stamping

When screen printing is not employed, printing on cloth (such as in the production of book covers) is most generally done with brass type using the process known as die-stamping. Conventional metal type is too soft for stamping jobs, where extra pressures are necessary, so brass type is better suited. Die-stamping can be done with conventional printing inks with satisfactory tack, but due to the uneven surfaces of some bookbinders' cloths, double impressions or "two hits" are sometimes necessary to get full coverage of the type or design image.

For particularly difficult or uneven surfaces, one must go beyond the use of inks and resort to foil. Foil is available in a variety of colors, as well as in metallics—gold, silver, and aluminum—and is available on plastic-backed sheets or strips, similar in form to a wide typewriter ribbon. Transferring the die image is brought about by applying pressure to the surface of the substrate with the foil sheet between the type and the base. Brass dies are usually heated to ensure a firm transfer of the foil. This requires a certain measure of control to avoid feathered edges or flaking of the foil, giving the type or image a ragged edge.

For a limited-run job, conventional lead type or an electro can be employed, but this, of course, does not permit the use of heat. As noted above, screen printing or even conventional offset printing can be used to transfer type or art designs to cloth, but the die-stamping technique tends to serve the purpose much better.

In recent years, foil die-stamping colors and finishes have been expanded and include copper tones, reds, blues, greens, pigment colors, dusted foils, and wood grains, and can be combined with other design techniques such as embossing and die-cutting. This process is also known as hot-leaf stamping and hot-foil stamping.

Finishing

While *bindery* is a broad term, *finishing* is even broader. The term encompasses almost every postpress operation performed by and in the bindery. In more finite terms, finishing can be limited to what some trade binderies refer to as "mounting and finishing," or the final preparation of displays. Since there is no clear-cut separation between bindery and finishing departments, we will deal with as many of these operations as can be readily defined and recognized.

Following are the major categories that fall under the general heading of finishing that have not been covered above.

Blind Stamping

Similar in process to the die-stamping technique covered earlier, blind stamping is the act of pressing a design into a base substrate, generally a book or pamphlet cover, with tools or dies, without the use of ink or foil, leaving only an impression—the reverse of embossing, which produces a raised design. As in die-stamping, a brass die is used to transfer the impression because of the amount of pressure required. Heavy-duty platen or vertical presses are used for this purpose.

Bookbinding

The art of bookbinding involves many steps after the printed pages or signatures are delivered to the bindery. High-speed techniques are used for sewing or adhering the signatures together and for covering or casing-in the finished, trimmed book block. Covers themselves range in quality and weight from heavy paper (cover stock) sometimes laminated or varnished for durability, to linen-finish cloth, buckram, vinyls, and the finest of tooled leathers in a variety of expensive skins (see chapter 11).

Case binding, or edition binding as it is frequently called, is distinguished by the hard-cover book with which we are most familiar.

Paperbacks, as the term implies, are cheaper versions of the edition books, often reprints, second printings, or texts where production economies are important to the publisher. Edition binding is one of the most complex of all tasks performed in a bindery, involving many steps. Thankfully, through the genius of technicians, most of the steps involved have been automated and are now performed by modern machinery.

After the printed book sheets or signatures are delivered from the press and are folded into the desired format sizes, usually in groups of 16- or 32-page units, multiple groups or signatures of consecutively numbered pages are combined and sewed or glued together at the backbone. Although gluing—or, more properly, plastic adhesion—is becoming more commonplace, sewing has had a long run of popularity. It has been used since the early days of hand stitching, and on through the development of specialty sewing machines, which still require a considerable amount of handwork.

Animal glue, once used in binding, had the unfortunate propensity of drying out and cracking when the book was opened, and also had a certain unpleasant odor. Today, any adhesive used is generally one of the more popular caseins, synthetic lactic, or rubber-based cements. Many types are made, in varying degrees of strength and with a far more acceptable aroma and elasticity.

After the individual book signatures are formed, the complete book block is assembled and sewn together, and endpapers are glued to the first and last page of the block. Before covers can be applied in the casing-in process, the books are subjected to a series of steps to ensure a flat, even product. These steps are known as *nipping* and *smashing*.

Nipping applies pressure to the backbone of the sewn book to reduce the swelling caused by the act of sewing. Smashing applies pressure to the entire surface of the book, which reduces each volume to a uniform thickness and removes the excess air from between the sheets or signatures. This is particularly important with books printed on a soft, matte-finished paper.

A final "gluing-off" step is necessary across the backbone of the book to fill any gaps between signatures and to strengthen the bind. This must be done carefully to avoid seepage of the glue between pages, which would cause them to stick together. With these elements of the book assembled, the time has come for trimming.

The book block is clamped securely on a trimming machine and is trimmed on three sides—head, foot, and front—with a three-knife trimmer. This operation not only smoothes the edges of the book but also frees the signature folds so the pages open readily. Some collector's-item books or special volumes are occasionally left untrimmed at the front edge to affect a ragged, deckle-edge design, necessitating the hand-slitting of some edges to free the pages.

Some books are left in a square-back block and are then essentially ready for covering. However, it is more desirable to "round and back" a book to give it a more finished appearance with a curved or concave front. All this is done on a single, high-speed binding machine, rounded with a set of rollers, then shaped with a backing iron. This procedure not only improves the appearance of the finished book but also protects the inner pages and extends the life of the book.

For added protection, and to provide a base for better cover adhesion, the rounded backbone of the book is layered with a piece of gauzelike crash material that is glued on and finally covered with a sheet of kraft liner. Finishing headbands are also applied at this step for a more decorative look. The crash extends beyond the edges of the book block to provide a hinge where the endpapers hold the book and the cover together. Casing-in the book is the next step.

A book cover is an assembly of binder's board (cardboard or chip board), lining material, and cover material, usually cloth, vinyl, or plastic. The cloth is fed from a continuous roll on the casing machine and is coated with adhesive. The boards, liner, and cardboard spine are placed on the cloth in the assembly, and the cloth is cut to the required length, with the corners being formed and glued.

In the final assembly, the book block is automatically carried to the opened cover, which is applied to the glued backbone. Building-in machines, with heated clamps and creasing irons, set the glue, and the finished product moves along a conveyor belt to a point where it may be wrapped with a preprinted book jacket before cartoning and mailing. Some books or sets of books may be further enclosed in a slip cover, a boxlike unit open at one side that provides for easy access to the books and for a more protective, dressy finish. The bookbinding process is a lengthy one, but thanks to automation the job can be completed faster than it takes to describe the operation.

Additional steps of refinement in the finishing of a book include thumb indexing, fancy gold-leaf edging sometimes used in the manufacture of Bibles and special books for collectors, embossing and stamping as previously described and, as is popular with paperbacks, edges painted with flamboyant colors. Marbling of edges, once popular on lawbooks and dictionaries, is still used on occasion but less often than it once was.

For the low-budget binding of pamphlets and paperbacks, adhesives are used to hold the signatures together in a hot-melt "perfect bind." This same technique is also used in assembling square-backed magazines and catalogs. Signatures are fed into a collator and are held together with a clamping device as they move along a bindery chain or conveyor. At one point, the spines or backbones of the signatures are passed through rotating blades that cut off the folded edges and rough them up with a series of saw-tooth wheels to create binding surfaces for the acceptance of an adhesive. After the roughing process the binding edge is coated with adhesive, the cover is affixed, and pressure is applied. The book block then passes through a three-knife trimmer and the binding process is complete.

Periodical Binding

Two major methods of periodical binding are in use today, saddle wire and the perfect bound hot-melt system as used with paperback books. Perfect binding is most popular with monthly publications or with the more bulky directories. Saddle wire is popular with the weekly magazines and smaller booklets, primarily because that method of binding tends to be faster than adhesive binding, although there has been a dramatic improvement in the speeds of the latter in recent years. Each type of binding has its advantages and disadvantages, as we shall see later. Sometimes it is a publisher's choice to elect one or the other method. Perfect-bound books have more of an appearance of permanence about them, and this binding method is selected for the thicker monthly publications.

In recent years, postal rates have skyrocketed for mailing all publications, so publishers have countered by reducing the basic weight of the paper used in their books. But lighter-weight stock tends to create problems in the bindery. Lightweight signatures are more apt to fold, crease, or flutter about in handling, particularly on the binding machine's conveyor chain. Manufacturers of bindery equipment are hard pressed to keep pace with controls to handle paper weights that have been reduced from 50 and 45 pounds down to 38 and 36 pounds. Now some of the more popular mass publications have dropped in weight to as little as 34 pounds and are experimenting with 32- and even 30-pound stock. Catalogs and directories, particularly, are often produced on the lighter papers.

For saddle-wire binding, signatures are usually delivered from the press with a ⅜-inch "binding lap" on the right-hand or high-folio side. This permits space for a gripper device on the gathering machine to grab one side of the signature and pull it over the conveyor chain so it can ride, in saddle fashion, down to the stitching heads.

The physical makeup of the binder/collator is such that many different signatures can be loaded into "pockets," or hoppers. They are laid out in a series of units on the machine, often in multiples of four. Also, they accommodate the complete assembly of a publication, consisting of a mix of individual signatures, color forms, and 8-, 12-, 16-, or 32-page units, with 4-page color units interspersed between them. If only one or two signatures are being assembled, as in a small booklet, the signatures may be fed by hand onto a smaller machine.

Today's large consumer magazines, with many different regional and demographic inserts to deal with, may require gathering or stitching machines with 30 or more hoppers. Signatures are fed automatically onto the conveyor chain via an intricate arrangement of grippers and suction cups that pull each signature from the bottom or side of the hopper stack, depending upon the design, make, or model of the machine. Some "closed-head" or front signatures can be folded without a gripper margin if the feeding mechanism on the gathering machine is equipped with the proper suction devices to draw the signature onto the chain.

For a multiple-signature publication, the hoppers are loaded progressively from the front, nearest the stitching heads with the publication cover. Then follows the signature to be bound right under the cover, and so back to the last unit, the center spread. In the assembly, the center spread drops over the chain first as it moves toward the stitcher head, with each successive signature being dropped on top of the one inside it, and the cover dropping on last.

The complete assembly of signatures, held in position by a stop bar, is then carried under the stitcher heads where staples, fed from a roll of wire, are pressed into the back margin of the book and are clinched inside the centerfold. Stitcher heads, usually in multiples of two or three, depending upon the thickness of the book and the amount of support needed to hold it firm, are positioned after the gathering assembly and before the trimmer. After stitching, the book continues along the conveyor and is fed, one or two books at a time, into a three-knife trimmer for finishing.

Because monthly publications tend to be thicker in number of pages, saddle stitching is not generally a satisfactory method for holding them together. Even some weeklies are, on occasion, so thick they would hold together better if they were perfect bound. But the concept of a weekly as a saddle-stitched book is so inbred in the minds of both readers and publishers that there is a reluctance to resort to perfect binding for them. Recently, however, one publisher of a popular weekly has elected to convert to the adhesive hot-melt system of binding, because his publication has grown so large.

As indicated earlier, there are advantages and disadvantages to each type of binding. Signatures for the saddle-stitch operation must be in units of four or more pages so they can ride the saddle chain conveyor. Perfect-bound pages, on the other hand, can readily be fed into the gathering machine as single leaves, printed two sides as a two-page unit. This can be a definite makeup advantage in some instances, specifically for "supplied forms," signatures supplied by a printer other than the one called upon to handle the final assembly and binding of the publication.

All modern publication-gathering machines are equipped with controls that can be operated from numerous positions along the assembly-line chain, so that the machine can be shut off quickly in the event of a jam-up. Lights over each hopper guide the operator to the trouble spot under such conditions. Furthermore, each machine is equipped with a sensor that "feels" the thickness of the assembled magazine, "kicking out" any incomplete books into a separate tray. These kick-outs can then be hand repaired. Other attachments, such as loose-card and bound-in card inserters, are available, as well as devices for tipping-in or tipping-on card units.

Today's automated bindery line is an all-in-one system. Conveyors or overhead cranes are replacing the hand-maneuvered skids of "parts" from the pressroom to the bindery. These stacks of signatures so conveyed are gravity-fed into the bindery machine hoppers with minor handwork necessary. At the end of the binding operation, an in-line mailing machine can be attached, or bundles of finished magazines can be tied or shrink wrapped. The mailing machine will attach labels to the magazine, sort by towns, bag, and tag in preparation for loading on skids or conveyors for delivery to the trucking platform and dispatch to distributors or post offices. Publications with exacting deadlines can thus move great volumes of product through their binderies in a most expeditious fashion.

Catalogs, directories, booklets, and smaller pamphlets, manufactured in quantity, can similarly be bound either by the perfect-bound or the saddle-stitched method, depending upon size or binding choice. Short-run publications can be readily handled on smaller, hand-fed stitchers and can be addressed and mailed on any one of a number of small machines designed for the small-quantity mailer.

Miscellaneous Binding

Many other forms of binding are available, including looseleaf peg, spiral, comb, and plastic. These all require some form of hole drilling or punching to accommodate the wire or plastic that holds the booklet together. This is referred to as mechanical binding and is frequently used for notebooks and other types of books that must open flat. Soft covers are best suited for mechanical binding, although added strength and protection can be offered by laminating or varnishing the cover. Sidewire binding, once a popular method of holding magazines and pamphlets together, has been almost completely replaced by perfect, hot-melt binds. While sidewire held a book together firmly, the pages were difficult to open and/or hold open, since so much of the back margin was committed to the staple area. For this type of bind, the cover was pasted on after the book was stapled, thus covering the stitch.

Following are a number of other binding and finishing methods:

Display Mounting

Large, poster-type displays are often printed directly onto a fairly heavy stock, but some are printed on paper and then mounted on heavier display boards with an adhesive. Unless they are to be inserted in display frames, easel backs can be applied for stand-alone display. This is a job for the bindery finishing department.

Easeling

Similar to mounting of displays, easeling is the act of attaching an easel prop or support to a poster or p-o-p display card to hold it erect. The easel stand itself is die-cut from cardboard in varying sizes and weights, depending upon the size of the poster or display it will have to support.

Embossing

The art of producing a raised design or lettering on paper or other substrate, embossing is accomplished by using matched relief and intaglio dies. The relief die is positioned beneath the paper and, under pressure, it forms a design as it is pressed into the hollow of the intaglio die above the paper. This process is the reverse of die-stamping. In neither case is ink ordinarily used; instead, the raised impression is relied on to carry the design effect. If an ink design is used, it is printed down in advance and the embossing is registered to the design. Blind embossing is done in a blank area where register is not important. Register embossing is more demanding and requires more care and make-ready.

Eyeletting

Eyelets are used to reinforce a punched hole in such specialty products as calendars, envelopes, and folders. They are usually made of metal and are pressed into the desired position with a special tool. This work is performed by companies specializing in mounting and finishing.

Flocking

This fanciful technique is used occasionally to decorate greeting cards and wrappings. Colored cotton fibers are dusted onto a surface where adhesive has been applied in a design pattern. The fibers are made to stand up, usually after being charged electrically, to create a velvety look. Sometimes the fibers are brushed for added effect.

Tin Edging

Calendars and wall charts frequently are supported or held together at the top with an inexpensive strip of tin, which is formed into a thin clamp. This holds pages together, as well as offering rigid support for hanging. The tinning clamp is formed by a simple clinching machine that squeezes the tin strip over the edges of the display or calendar pages, thereby acting as a binder. At the same time, a flat tin eyelet hook is applied for hanging.

In addition to the above, there are literally hundreds of custom finishing jobs performed by machine or, in many cases, by hand in the bindery. This is truly a catch-all department, capable of many unusual chores. When in doubt in planning a job that may call for some unusual form of treatment, contact your bindery foreman. He or she can suggest ways and means of getting your job done cheaper and faster, and in many cases will supply solutions to problems that were thought to be unsolvable.

How to Use 15
Direct Mail

So you're thinking about using direct mail. Fine idea—but have you realized the range of formats, as well as the variety of marketing, advertising, and promotion functions subsumed under that single heading?

Direct mail, from the point of view of physical format, can consist of anything from a simple postcard to a series of "dimensional" mailings. As an example, a dimensional series, which was created some time ago for Union Carbide, included such items as a pure silk scarf with gold and silver threads, along with personalized letters from the president of Union Carbide to the presidents of their present and potential customers.

Direct mail also includes brochures and self-mailers of various degrees of complexity, as well as catalogs. The latter vary from small black-and-white affairs to multi-hundred-page merchandise offerings printed in full color by offset, gravure, or both. They often vary in content according to the geographical location and buying history of the recipient and can be imprinted with his or her name, address, and account number, as well as a special message keyed to any special interests.

The first question for the potential user of direct mail is, "What goal do I intend to accomplish?"

Marketing Aspects of Direct Mail

Direct mail is an *advertising medium* in the same way that television, radio, newspapers, magazines, or billboards are. (For more on advertising and promotion, see chapter 1.) From the marketing point of view, there are two main purposes that direct mail serves efficiently: *sales promotion* and *direct marketing* (also known as *mail-order selling*).

Your marketing objective will largely determine which of the infinite variety of formats permitted in direct mail are appropriate. For this reason, these marketing factors will be discussed briefly before proceeding to the discussion of formats and their production.

When used as a sales promotion tool, direct mail supports general advertising and selling activity, rather than closing the sale itself. Typical examples are announcements of new products or special sales and, most importantly, the generation and qualification of sales leads.

Not many years ago, in pre-OPEC days, traveling salespeople crisscrossed the continent, calling on even comparatively small business and industrial accounts regularly and frequently. But for most manufacturers this is no longer possible.

Not only are fewer qualified sales representatives to be had but the cost of keeping them on the road has risen dramatically. According to the Laboratory of Advertising Performance, McGraw-Hill Research, by 1985 the cost of the average industrial sales call had risen to $229.70, within some industries much higher.

Those figures do not show the cost of a sale, but merely of a single sales *call*. Since, in most industries, from three to six calls are required to close an average sale, it can readily be seen that the cost of making a sale by unaided personal selling may well approach or even exceed $1,400.

That is why direct mail as sales promotion plays so vital a role today. Survey after survey has proved that prior preparation by mail makes sales calls more effective—several times so, when they are made as a result of a request by the prospect via the reply card from a mailing.

Here is the basic reason why direct mail can profitably employ expensive techniques and utilize high-priced items as goodwill builders—*provided* that those techniques and products are properly tied in to the marketing objective and advertising theme. At the same time, they must be directed only to the proper decision-makers in precisely those organizations that are the prime prospects for the advertiser's products or services.

The intent here is not to discuss in detail the highly sophisticated techniques that have been developed to pinpoint the proper recipients, as well as to qualify all leads prior to turning them over to the sales force. Suffice it to say that in many instances, two-tiered direct mail lead-getting programs, combined with proper mail lead qualification, have resulted in seven-figure increases in net sales profit *after* all expenses, with no increase in the size of the field sales-force.

Sales-promotion uses of direct mail also include maintaining contact with customers between visits by field personnel; keeping customers informed of new product uses; and building awareness and acceptance of, and preference for, your brand as opposed to your competitors'.

The second major function of direct mail—direct marketing, or mail-order selling—is completely different. Whereas sales promotion strives to pave the way for the salesperson and to make his or her time more productive, direct marketing eliminates the salesperson completely. Its format is often determined by the nature of the products offered and the demographics and psychographics of the audience. Increasingly, it is being utilized not only in selling consumer goods but also in business-to-business sales. Many of America's largest industrial firms, which experimented first with mail-order selling of supplies and comparatively low-priced equipment, have found that direct marketing provides a solution to the problem of selling their machines profitably to smaller companies.

The Cost-effectiveness of Direct Mail

How do you determine the cost-effectiveness of a direct-mail package? *Encyclopedia Britannica,* one of the largest users of direct mail, presents a good example. They use the mails primarily for sales-lead development, measuring the number of leads and the number of closings from each type of mailing. Note that counting leads alone is not enough, since it is conceivable that one type of mailing might develop more leads by creating an incorrect impression of a product, thus making the salesperson's job more difficult and reducing the number of closings. (Naturally, any mailer so sophisticated as *Encyclopedia Britannica* would be unlikely to approve a misleading copy theme; but stranger things have happened than a failure to recognize how one particular group of prospects will interpret language.)

Where the purpose of your mailing is to generate actual sales rather than leads, the calculation of cost-effectiveness involves many factors. For a preliminary estimate, work backwards: compute the cost per thousand in the mail, and divide by the order margin (the difference between selling price and all costs of the sale other than promotion cost). That will give you the number of units that must be sold per thousand in order to break even.

But even if you cannot reasonably anticipate selling that many units, your mailing may still prove profitable. The great benefit in securing customers through the mails is that clients obtained by such a low-pressure sales technique as direct mail tend to remain customers (assuming, of course, that you give them good value and service). Thus, many firms find that they can afford to pay comparatively large sums to get a new customer.

They compute the *lifetime value* of a customer by multiplying the profit margin on an average sale by the number of times an average purchaser buys before becoming inactive. They then know how much they can afford to spend to buy a new customer. (Of course, this is a gross oversimplification. Many factors affect the purchasing profile, among them the medium through which the new name was obtained—the specific publication, TV outlet, or mailing list; the offer; the size of the first purchase; and so on. But the principle remains valid.)

Creativity in Direct Mail

Success in direct mail—of whichever variety— requires three elements: the right product, the right market, and the right creative approach.

Just as it is within the range of possibility, but very difficult, to make use of a three-legged stool that has only two functioning legs, direct-mail success calls for all three of those vital supports. Discussion of the product and the market (the mailing list) are beyond the scope of this volume, but creativity—since it determines the type and shape of the pieces that must be produced—is decidedly to the point.

Creative directors have a broader range of options in direct mail than in any other advertising medium, without exception. Television is *not* an exception, since records, films, cassettes, and videodiscs have all been employed as elements in direct-mail campaigns. These four media have frequently been featured in sales promotion (phonograph records for selling books and magazines and for fund-raising—a form of direct marketing—as well). Sears Roebuck has distributed many thousands of videodiscs, each carrying the equivalent of an entire mail-order catalog in addition to "live" demonstrations of a wide range of merchandise.

Is there, then, no limit to creativity in direct mail? Physically, there is indeed none; the creative director of a mail program can appeal to every sense and use every product and material in the process. But there must be one restriction on the application of invention to direct mail: Every penny spent must justify itself by adding considerably more than that amount to the net profit derived from the program.

Emphatically, this does not mean that your mailing pieces should be as inexpensive as possible. *Encyclopedia Britannica,* after years of insisting that "less is more" and using mailings consisting of little more than a brief letter and a reply card, reversed its field . . . and found that money spent in creating well-thought-out, elaborate mailing packages was wisely invested.

There is only one way to overcome the effects of constant cost increases in the "three P's"—paper, printing, and postage—and that is to *invest more in creativity,* to find new ways to increase the productivity of your mailings.

In working to that end, your creative personnel, whether in-house or employed by a direct-response agency or consultants, can make use of all the following elements:

Time
Yes, *time;* repetition pays in building awareness of your message, which must be reinforced before the previous impression has passed out of your prospect's mind. Proper timing and the correct number of mailings in a given sales-promotion program are too idiosyncratic to permit general rules. Test, test, and test again.

Color
Use it to make sales points, if it is appropriate to your product and your audience. But remember that the understated, personalized letter (whatever the production process) is for many purposes, especially to executives, the most effective type of mail promotion.

The tasteful employment of a second color will often secure greater readership and response. Beyond that point, the next practical stage is four-color process (unless you are contemplating a comic-book-style approach or a newsprint flier, when four flat colors can be appropriate). Process color increases the preparatory costs to a considerable degree and is therefore beyond the budget of many small advertisers, especially when the potential audience is comparatively small. It can bring large benefits in the long run, however, and in a wide range of uses, through its ability to portray products and scenes in full, natural tonal range.

Size

Printed materials used in direct-mail promotion are limited only by the size of the largest press available. Reproductions of artwork, posters, "bedsheet"-size brochures—all can be employed. You are not restricted by the ability to insert your piece within the binding of a magazine or other medium.

Three-Dimensional Pieces

Three-foot-long kites, old-time trainmen's lanterns, model railroad trains, foot-high aluminum chess sets, busts of Nefertiti and of Tutankhamen are among the unusual products that have served as theme elements in direct-mail sales-promotion programs. When the "dimensionals" fit properly in the sales theme, they can produce not only an increase in sales but also much favorable word-of-mouth promotion.

Sound

Some of the more elaborate uses of sound in direct mail, such as recording an entire catalog on a videodisc, have already been described. It is possible to make use of sound less expensively, however. The sounds of the Old West, for example, can be recreated on a flexible plastic record, to help put the prospect in the mood to buy a set of "wild west" books, especially if an exciting excerpt from one volume is recorded on the reverse.

Scent

"Scratch-and-sniff" and similar techniques enable the direct-mail advertiser to provide the actual scent of a perfume, the aroma of fresh fruit, or other elements that will increase the probability of buying. Alternatively, the entire mailing package can be exposed to the essence of coffee or of a wood fire.

Texture

Research has demonstrated that the employment of textured paper stock, perhaps of an ivory tint, can improve response over that received by the identical mailing on white offset paper. But you can go far beyond the use of textured paper: create contrasts between metallic surfaces and leatherlike printing media, for example—*provided* that the contrasts are appropriate to, and do not draw attention away from, your sales story. (For more on the varieties and selection of papers, see chapter 11.)

That caveat cannot be repeated too often regarding all phases of creativity in direct mail—and, in fact, in all advertising: advertising creativity must always remain the servant of its primary function, which is to advance the sale of a product or service.

Direct-Mail Formats

The formats you employ, as well as your marketing approach and the copy and art, can actually defeat your purposes if not properly chosen. Formats provide the "stage setting" for your sales message; they must be appropriate to it.

Look through any book on direct mail published more than 10 years ago, and you will probably find a list of mailing formats, each well defined and easily distinguished from the others. It is no longer possible to categorize formats so neatly, since the development of ink-jet and laser printing (see chapter 18).

These techniques, in theory at least, would permit the printing of every copy of a book in a different size and style of type to suit the preference of the individual reader. When combined with computer-controlled printing and bindery equipment (see chapter 14), they allow virtually unlimited selection of segments of a catalog to be mailed to each customer, with the buyer's name, address, and account number imprinted on the order form and on a message especially tailored to increase that sale.

Today, as a result of these new production processes, one would be hard put to declare categorically that a given piece of direct mail is a self-mailer, a letter, a brochure, or, indeed, a combination of all of these. An increasing number of specialty printers can process various types of combination mailers. Their facilities and abilities vary—

one more reason why it is important to consult with the printer you intend to use *before* you make final plans for, much less design and write, your mailing.

Do such complex mailing packages actually get read? Yes, definitely, if they are attractive, well written, and keyed to the interests of the recipient.

When the first ink jet came on the scene, it seemed to many people to be enough to insert the recipient's name, several times, in different styles and sizes of type, with a reference or two to "your neighbors in _____" or "in front of your door at _____." The very newness of the method made this work for a while, although in many cases it was ludicrous for an address in a large metropolitan area.

Fortunately, computer programs have become far more sophisticated, permitting the inclusion of many elements (such as the names and ages of children, the school name and year, the specific types of previous purchases). Now these processes demand of the copywriter not only true creativity but also complete marketing knowledge, in order to employ the new capabilities wisely.

Many of the computer-controlled formats can be almost ridiculously inexpensive, provided that the print run is large enough. Often, however, it takes millions of pieces to reach the low-cost point. Setup costs on the complicated equipment required can make tests quite expensive, and no two suppliers' facilities are identical. Check at the start!

Despite the proliferation of new, proprietary computerized mailing formats, the tenets of the basic "Format A" for subscription and book selling, as well as for many "solo" (only one product promoted) mailings, remain:

- a strong selling letter, often four pages long;
- a brochure or broadside, from 11 by 17 inches up to 35 by 45 inches;
- an order form, possibly with a "token," stamps, or other device to promote action;
- frequently, a second or "lift" letter;
- a business reply envelope; and the whole enclosed in
- a carrying envelope, either 6 by 9 inches, 9 by 12 inches, or #10, usually imprinted with a sales message.

This basic mailing format can be likened in many ways to the "Layout A" for full-page print ads, brought to its highest form by the advertising agency Doyle Dane Bernbach some 30 years ago: the square or nearly-square photo occupying more than half the total area, then a concise headline, followed by a moderate-sized copy block surrounded by white space. The similarity occurs because novice advertisers are less likely to go wrong if they adhere to the "standard" rather than striving for originality in format. Yet every day, someone achieves success by being different—but only if that difference arises out of the marketing story, rather than competing with it.

Format A of direct mail, by its very nature, allows more variation within itself than does print advertising's Layout A. The most frequently encountered variation is the addition of a second brochure or broadside, to emphasize a particular feature of the advertised product.

Another means of making your package different—but one that is becoming less effective as it is more and more widely employed—is the substitution of a plastic wrap for the paper envelope. The role of the designer is of major importance here, since it can make or break the whole mailing; poorly designed or manufactured plastic covers, or those of cheap-looking materials, can destroy the high-quality feeling you have spent so much time, effort, and money to achieve.

At their best, plastic envelopes can focus attention on a colorful element within, sometimes at a lower cost than either a "billboard window" envelope—one on which nearly the entire flat side of the envelope is of cellophane or other transparent material—or a standard envelope on which the same colorful material has also been printed. If you plan to use a plastic wrap, save yourself headaches by insisting on seeing the printer's samples of the exact type and gauge of plastic, method of manufacture, and style and quality of printing you will be given.

Extra attention-getting power can be created by the appropriate use of die-cutting on the brochure and the order device, or both. This technique involves extra cost, however, which may be greater than the boost in response, particularly if your designer is not fully aware of paper and press sizes.

Elements of Direct Mail

Keeping all these factors in mind, then, and remembering that it is not always possible to draw lines of distinction among these formats, here are brief descriptions of the more frequently encountered types of mailings.

The letter remains the most important single element in virtually every mail advertising program, whether for sales promotion or mail-order selling. In some specialized cases, such as catalogs, the letter can be placed on a "wraparound" or incorporated within the catalog itself. Generally, however, the letter should remain a separate element within the mailing package, especially in mail designed to generate sales leads.

Tests have compared the power of "straight" letters versus illustrated letters versus illustrated folders in securing business sales leads. Although art ideally suited to both the product and the prospect will get results, in the great majority of the tests the more personal-appearing plain letter has topped the field.

Almost every day, it seems, another method of producing personalized letters is developed. Very few lettershops still maintain facilities to produce multigraphed letters, which are printed on a small rotary press from movable type through an inked ribbon and then filled in with name and address on a typewriter. Many more plants now offset a letter with a special black ink, which matches the typewriter ribbon used to fill in the name and address with the typeface used for the offset reproduction of the body of the letter.

Both these processes can result in a letter that appears to be individually typed. Because of low preparatory cost, the processes are useful for short-run, individualized letters. If you have word-processing equipment, you can, of course, produce individualized letters in runs of various lengths (see chapter 16).

If you plan to have computer letters printed commercially, insist on seeing samples first. Quality ranges from superb down to virtually unacceptable, although the worst are being driven to upgrade by the pressure of competition. Also, check the program carefully, to ensure that it can handle all the idiosyncrasies of your project. One no longer sees many computer letters addressed to attorneys as "Dear Mr. Esq.," but how does the program deal with such ambiguous first names as Pat or Leslie?

A number of producers have special machinery that permits both computer personalization of the letter and a reply form, as well as computer printing of the name and address on the same sheet of paper, which is then cut off and folded automatically into an envelope. This eliminates completely the risk of incorrect insertions, as with A's letter landing in B's envelope. Some machinery also permits automatic insertion of from one to three enclosures at the same time.

Again, variations in specifications (size of letter, amount of personalization, style of envelope) make it absolutely essential that you check with your suppliers *before* you begin planning. In this instance in particular, be sure you are satisfied with the style of envelope the supplier can manufacture. Some machines will supply envelopes with seams that are square rather than diagonal, which looks quite attractive; others produce an envelope with perforated edges.

Whatever type of letter you decide to use (and it often pays to test the respective pulling power, for your particular offer, of two or more types), remember that letters are the most personal, and potentially the most effective, form of mail communication; they are also the most personal form of selling, short of a face-to-face visit.

Do not be fooled into thinking that writing a sales letter is easy—whether its purpose is to secure a request for more information or an appointment, or to make an outright sale. The sales letter is often the most difficult part of a mail package to write; one word or phrase out of key can cut the results—even to zero.

The folder, frequently called a *flier* or a *circular,* is a printed piece, folded but not bound into a multipage format. Its size customarily ranges between 8½ by 11 inches (standard letterhead size) and 17 by 22 inches; when oversize, the term *broadside* or (an insider's term) *bedsheet* is applied to it, and occasionally, *brochure.* Folders are effective when it is appropriate to convey the impression of a low-cost, no-frills operation or of a rushed, almost emergency situation.

In most instances, a folder should not be asked to carry your whole sales story. Employ it as backup to the letter accompanying it; let it reinforce your sales points by citing benefits more completely and using photos and art to build conviction.

When a flier is mailed alone, without an envelope, it is called a *self-mailer.* If you intend your flier to be subjected to that use, be sure you print it on a sturdy stock—an index, tag, or bristol—unless the number of folds gives it the bulk to withstand postal abuse. Check with your local postmaster before designing it to be sure it has the required closed sides and the legal area for addressing and postal indicia.

The booklet, sometimes (especially in its more elaborate forms) called the *brochure,* is physically similar to the folder except that it has been subjected to one more production operation, having been trimmed and either stapled, glued, or (in larger booklets) sewn into a number of same-size pages. The benefits are twofold: the reader is guided step by step through your sales story, and, especially in the case of larger brochures with a separate cover, a feeling of importance and dignity can be created that tends to give the brochure longer life than many other printed pieces.

On the other hand, the booklet is often less effective than a broadside in generating excitement and immediate action. Because of the binding, also, and where a separate cover is used, its unit cost is higher.

The catalog is distinguishable from the brochure more by its contents than its form. Whereas the brochure is employed to disseminate information, instructions, or opinions, the catalog is basically a listing of all (or a great many of) the products produced or sold by its issuer and is often intended to prompt direct sales. Although catalogs can be as simple as a single sheet, they usually vary from 24 to several hundred pages, 5½ by 8½ inches or 8½ by 11 inches in size.

Frequency of Mailings

In sales promotion particularly, repetitive mailings are usually necessary for greatest effect. This is, of course, true in all advertising, regardless of the medium employed. The optimal frequency of your mailings depends partly upon the nature of the buying pattern for your product and partly upon the importance of the prospects addressed in your overall sales plan. Prime prospects are often addressed at least monthly, with three mailings at two-week intervals at the start of the program to establish name recognition.

Most mailers find that a family resemblance—in theme, if not always in format—is beneficial. Preempting a particular approach, style, or sales argument can be valuable. On the other hand, an occasional radical change, to boost possibly flagging attention, has its proponents.

Some industrial sales promotional mailings have proceeded in an uninterrupted series, every month, for decades. Over the years, a continuing mail contact program may elicit a response of some sort (not necessarily an actual order or a request for a salesperson to call) from virtually every name on the prospect list. It can be invaluable in establishing your firm as one worthy of being included on the bidding list for major equipment, for example.

Where your aim is to secure actual sales through the medium of your mailings, the question of follow-ups takes a different form. In a number of cases (especially when selling expensive consumer items) the initial mailing makes a sale at a profit. Usually, however, it costs money to add an active buyer name to your list. That fact should make it evident that follow-up mailings—offers to sell additional products to your newly acquired customers—are essential. And the sooner you ask for more business, the more money you will make.

If you send an acknowledgment of the order, include a "special" or premium with it. Publishers often convert short-term trials to long-term subscribers at that point. Enclose information on related products—even another copy of your catalog, if the initial order was generated from it—in the package when you fulfill the order. Try using the telephone to say thank you, at which time you may get an add-on order at the same time, too. Sending an additional copy of your catalog six to eight weeks after the first often generates greater volume and prolongs its life cycle. Later, you can send it again, this time perhaps with a new cover and a shift in the order of the printed signatures.

How often you can profitably mail to your active customers varies from industry to industry and firm to firm. Frequently, sophisticated mail-order merchants address catalogs to the most profitable segments of their list eight to eleven times a year.

The Lettershop

This chapter would not be complete without a few remarks on that strange beast, the lettershop; chances are that you will have to deal with one. Determine what services are most important to you before making a choice, since virtually no two are alike in their range of capabilities.

Lettershops sprang up in the last decades of the nineteenth century with the invention of machines such as the already-described multigraph, which made it possible to produce "personal" letters in quantity. Such shops customarily handled not only the production of letters and other small printed pieces but also insertion—all by hand—and mailing.

As machinery grew in complexity and specialization, so did lettershops, many of which began to call themselves mailing houses. Some only accepted large-volume mailings; others built a mailing-list capability, now usually on computer, that can often save you money through lowered postal rates. Still other shops grew into huge printing establishments or complete fulfillment and warehousing centers. Pay your money and take your chances, but beware of the too-low-to-be-possible estimate—it usually does not include some necessary step or item.

Because the lettershop is the final stage in production, it is often blamed for the faults of preliminary suppliers. No one can mail 250,000 "packages," for example, if the envelope house delivered only 248,000—or an even 250,000, for that matter, since you must allow for machine spoilage. A really good lettershop will keep you informed of late deliveries and potential problems with your other suppliers if you have made clear to them, in writing, exactly what to expect, when, and from where.

Complete and detailed schedules should be set up and watched closely by both your in-house traffic manager and the account executive, production assistant, or whoever is your primary contact inside the shop. Insist on being assigned such a contact person; indeed, make it a point to get to know him or her before you assign your work to that shop. (For more on planning procedures, see chapter 12.)

Try to avoid the most-requested mailing dates, such as the week after Christmas. If you must mail at a very busy period, you might reserve time on the lettershop's machinery months ahead; but if you do, expect to be billed for the time if your material is not completely ready on the agreed date.

Direct mail, of whatever variety, is handled in so many ways by different companies that no simple statement can cover the responsibilities of those concerned with its production. Some firms do everything from creation to printing and preparation for mailing in-house; others have extensive production facilities but rely on ad agencies, specialized direct-marketing agencies, or consultants for ideas, art, copy, and mechanicals.

There is, however, one rule that applies universally: *one* person within your organization must have full responsibility for scheduling, including seeing to it that all internal departments and external suppliers, creative or mechanical, perform on time. Only in that manner can you assure yourself of top direct-mail results.

Word 16
Processing

Printing almost always includes the reproduction of text or copy of some sort. How and by whom the actual words are written varies, but they are usually in typewritten form if they are to be typeset (typesetting is covered in chapter 9). To make the route from writer to typesetter more efficient, the technology of electronic word processing has achieved great success. Some systems even eliminate "hard" typewritten copy, with all writing and editing done on a video screen and sent digitally to the typesetter. In addition to saving human time and energy, word-processing hardware and software are now affordable for large and small businesses. The investment in word-processing equipment or services can allow users to produce certain printed pieces such as form letters in-house, rather than contracting the job to a commercial printer.

What Is Word Processing?

A word processor is a specific unit of hardware, operated with word-processing software, that allows the mechanical processing of words—text or copy. Dedicated word-processing systems (separate from larger computer systems) either stand alone or are operated as part of a multiunit system. Word-processing programs are now available for many models of personal computers as well.

As words wind their way from the mind of an author to the printed page, they undergo more than one metamorphosis. The author goes through one or more rewrites; the editors change and modify; the typesetter proofreads and corrects; the author makes alterations. Finally, the finished pages are ready to be photographed, stripped, plated, printed, cut, collated, bound, and shipped.

If we think about all of the words and all of the things that happen to those words from mind to matter, then it is possible to envision a sort of electronic word bank in which those words can be deposited initially. From there they go through an infinite number of editing cycles from the author to the editors to the typesetter to the lawyers or whomever. The technology necessary to make this concept workable is here, now, in word processing. The elements that allow it to pass from the blue sky to solid earth are (1) the ability to input (record) information via a device that is essentially typewriter oriented, with correction and modification functions during input, and (2) the ability to retrieve information from the recorded medium for successive editing and re-storage. To summarize, word processing makes possible the electronic input, storage, retrieval, editing, and re-storage of text information.

Input is the conversion of information from a human-understandable state to a machine-understandable state. An input device, such as a typewriter, performs this function. For example, when you type, you hit a key that begins a series of operations, mostly mechanical, to select the right character for impression on the paper.

A word processor links a magnetic recording device, usually a memory disk these days, to the typewriter and simultaneously records the information and/or outputs (prints) the text. The important part of the input operation is the capturing or recording of the information as early in the evolution of the word bank as possible.

Input has always been a redundant operation; after many revisions and retypings, copy is usually rekeyed to record it for typesetting. Such redundant input introduces the opportunity for creating new errors that must be found and corrected. A word processor allows the user to input information once and then edit it electronically, thereby reducing error generation and speeding up the editing and typesetting cycles. Whereas input used to imply typing on the keyboard of a Linotype machine, now it can mean typing on a word processor's keyboard to gain the same results.

Word-processing Functions

Word-processing functions can be divided into four main areas: (1) *document creation,* used to enter text via a video terminal; (2) *editing functions,* used to correct and amend previously entered documents; (3) *formatting functions,* used to prepare edited documents for output by various letter-quality and/or high-speed printers; and (4) *utility functions,* used to store, copy, and merge documents and for printer control. Advanced functions include general programming features for integrating variable and preformatted text and many special routines for mathematics, graphics, mailing, filing, and appointment scheduling.

Document Creation

Commands are designed to make document composition at the keyboard as simple as possible. A user formats using a "menu," displayed on the screen, which allows the user to "order" such functions as tabs, left and right margins, page breaks, paragraph indents, and spacing. On most systems, a user can invoke a "word-wrap" function that acts like an automatic carriage return on a typewriter. The word-wrap function moves any word that crosses the right-hand margin to the next line and adjusts all subsequent text. The function keeps up with even the fastest typists and speeds input, since the user need not note the end of a line.

Scrolling and cursor-control functions further speed data entry. Scrolling allows the users to move all text up and down, either a line at a time or a page at a time. Cursor-control keys allow a text to be moved left and right or up and down, by character, word, and tab stop, also by line and page. Other functions move the cursor to the top or bottom of the screen, to the beginning or end of a document, to the start of the next line (return), or to the start of the next page.

Editing Functions

A user can insert spaces, characters, words, phrases, and blocks of text anywhere in a document; just as easily accomplished is the deletion of spaces, characters, words, full and partial lines, paragraphs, and pages. Selective delete commands can erase everything from the cursor to the end of a document or up to or including a specified character.

Block operations work on areas of text, defined by special characters called block indicators. Once defined, blocks can be copied, moved, deleted, printed or stored.

Search-and-replace operations work on word and letter combinations called strings. A user can find a string and, if necessary, replace it with another string. Such operations can be performed individually, repeated, or performed automatically. Search-and-delete commands are also possible. A global search-and-replace command performs a specified operation on every occurrence of a string within a document. "Wild card" operations use special characters to find similar strings.

Formatting
In most word-processing packages, formatting functions take advantage of full-function printers. Once a document has been entered and revised, the user formats it by filling in a checklist of formatting options. Page formats are specified in terms of right, left, top, and bottom margins, characters per inch, lines per inch, paragraph spacing, and physical page length. The user can, for instance, request automatic page headings and automatic roman or arabic page numbers printed in any location or alternating between right- and left-hand corners for "book-style" arrangements. Special format options allow the user to number paragraphs, force new pages, and permit two-column printing.

Justification options are numerous as well. Right, left, and right-and-left justification are almost universally available, as are line- and page-centering commands. Three newer justification options are hard (unsplittable) spaces for phrases that should not be split by right margins, hard hyphens, which are similar, and automatic alignment of columnar decimal data.

Numerous character attributes, which most word-processing software can specify, take advantage of today's multifunction printers. Characters can be boldfaced, underlined, superscripted, subscripted, overprinted, and printed in a second color (using a two-color ribbon). Such attributes can be used individually or in a combination.

Utility Functions
These allow the user to save documents for future editing and printing, maintain document libraries, and often generate automatic backup files. These functions can delete partial, total, and multiple files and can link and merge files to build documents from pieces of other documents.

Printer-control functions allow users to print partial, single, and multiple documents, often during editing and document creation. Pause commands allow users to change ribbons, paper, and printwheels during a print run, and conversion routines convert upper- or lowercase characters to the opposite case.

One of the features inherited from the printing and publishing industry is the "what you see is what you get" video screen that displays justified, proportionally spaced, enhanced text in finished page formats, complete with headings and page numbers, on the screen just as they will appear in printed form. To make things even easier, more and more word-processing software packages include automatic index and table of contents generators, as well as spelling and syntax checker/correctors.

A History of Word Processing

Word processing traces its ancestry back to the typewriter, the mechanical device that revolutionized the office in the first decade of this century. Up until that time, office correspondence had been handled by legions of handwriting copyists. The typewriter allowed an average typist to outperform the best copyist.

The next step in the evolution of word processing came with automatic typewriters in the 1930s. These machines could repetitively type form letters and contracts, using a perforated paper roll, a "storage" mechanism similar to those found on player pianos. The typewriter was enhanced in the 1950s by electricity, the addition of punched paper tape as a storage medium, and electromechanical logic, which allowed switching between multiple tape units. These machines could be applied to repetitive tasks, which also involved a degree of searching, selecting, and merging text stored on the punched paper tape.

In 1964, International Business Machines (IBM) coupled computer technology with the Selectric typewriter in the design of the Magnetic Tape Selectric Typewriter (MT/ST), a magnetic tape cartridge typing system, which ushered in word processing as we know it.

The MT/ST magnetic tape could be erased and re-recorded; punched paper tape could not. The MT/ST tape was therefore more compact, having a storage density of about 20 characters per inch versus 6 characters per inch for paper tape. Magnetic tape cartridges could be handled and stored more efficiently than paper tape, and transport search/retrieval speeds on magnetic tape systems were also faster.

In 1969, IBM introduced the Magnetic Card Selectric Typewriter (MC/ST)—a word-processing typewriter that employed a reusable, page-oriented magnetic card as a recording medium. The page orientation of this word processor was easy for typewriter operators to conceptualize, and the MC/ST met with high acceptance. The popularity of this model made it the standard to which all other word processors were matched. For example, in 1971, Redactron introduced a line of magnetic-card and magnetic-tape typewriters; the magnetic-card version was compatible with the IBM version.

The 1970s witnessed accelerated activity in word processing. Lexitron (now Raytheon) and Linolex (now 3M) introduced the first video display systems in 1972. Concurrently, Comptek Research was among the first to offer a shared-logic, multikeyboard computer system dedicated to word-processing tasks. Vydec became the first manufacturer to incorporate magnetic recording diskettes with a video-based word processor in 1973. These technological milestones were coupled with the entry of many new companies into the market, including Olivetti (1971); CPT and Wang (1972); Savin (1973); Royal and Xerox (1974); A.B. Dick, Lanier, and Digital Equipment (1976); and AM Jacquard (1977).

In 1980 IBM's Display Writer was introduced. It set a new competitive standard for hardware and software modularity, at a price under $10,000. At the same time, Syntrex introduced a system that offered a range of products from the lowest end to the highest end, including large amounts of storage, electronic filing, and many advanced functions; this further solidified the need for other vendors to market a full range of products. With the introduction of the 8010 Star, Xerox began selling a product aimed at professional workers; the company also announced the implementation of Ethernet, an electronic network that could link electronic office equipment together. The emergence of computer manufacturers such as Honeywell, Prime Computer, and Burroughs, as well as personal-computer manufacturers such as Apple and Radio Shack, gave increased impetus to low-cost text editing. More than 50 companies are now involved in the direct—and more recently dealer and retail—marketing of word-processing equipment, and new vendors are entering the marketplace on a regular basis.

Word-processing Products

Word-processing products can be classed in three broad categories: (1) stand-alone (or dedicated) systems; (2) multiterminal systems; and (3) personal computers that operate word-processing software.

A stand-alone word processor consists of a single work-station that contains its own control logic. Within this classification are contained a number of different units.

Electronic Typewriters

Best described as the electronic equivalent of the electric or mechanical typewriter, these emerged in 1978 when Qyx introduced its Intelligent Typewriter. Eventually every typewriter will be an electronic typewriter, taking its place at the low end of the word-processing market as a logical upgrade for existing users of electric typewriters. They are generally intended for the secretary's desk rather than in the word-processing center. Though not full-fledged word processors, electronic typewriters feature small memories for minimal text or phrase storage and recall; these devices also incorporate a number of features such as automatic centering, automatic numeral alignment, automatic underlining, and automatic carrier return, which facilitate the keyboarding and revision of small amounts of text on a limited basis. There is no removable recording medium, although this type of feature is anticipated in the future.

Stand-alone Mechanical Word Processors

These consist of an integral keyboard/printer (usually a modified typewriter) that is coupled with edit and control logic, internal memory, and an auxiliary magnetic media recorder (card, cassette, tape cartridge, or diskette). The keyboard and printer are actually the typewriter, used to generate text for editing operations as well as for final printout. A stand-alone mechanical word-processor can range in price from $3,000 to more than $10,000. Though not representing the current state-of-the-art in word-processing technology and capability, stand-alone mechanical systems are still widely used.

Stand-alone "Thin-Window" Display Units

Consisting of an integral keyboard/printer and a one-line or partial-line video display, these units afford a "window" into memory. Such systems ease editing tasks and offer the operator a series of visual cues during the text entry and editing processes. Olivetti and Artec were the first firms to enter this market; Xerox joined in 1977 with the Display Typewriter. In 1978 Qyx and A.B. Dick entered the "thin-window" marketplace. A.B. Dick introduced the Magna II that same year.

Stand-alone Video-based Word Processors

These replace the keyboard/printer with a separate keyboard, as well as a video display screen, single or dual media drives (usually diskette), and a separate printer. With this type of word-processing configuration, text is keyed, edited, and changed on the screen before printout. Some models may be equipped to perform a number of integrated functions, such as data processing, electronic mail, administrative support, and personal computing. Stand-alone video-based word processors are priced from under $10,000 to over $20,000, the higher-priced versions offering data processing and other capabilities.

These word processors have internal or buffer memory systems capable of holding several display pages of text. Such extra capacity allows lines of text to be viewed for editing, updating, and revision, and allows the addition of new text to a document file. Text is either "called up" from memory files stored on magnetic media (usually diskette) or input directly into the machine.

Dual-media station (dual card, dual cassette, dual diskette, and so on) word processors have more flexibility than their single-medium counterparts. Card-to-card, tape-to-tape, or disk-to-disk operations are possible. New or revised text can be input and merged with existing files, printed out, and then remain stored. For example, address lists and individualized data can be combined with prestored, repetitive information to generate "customized" form letters; new additions to such address lists may also be collated onto a master file. However, such tasks on single-medium word processors are less automatic and usually require more direct operator intervention.

Multiterminal Word-processing Systems

These configurations incorporate more than one work-station, where these stations share one or more particular computer or storage resource. Included in this broad category of equipment are shared-logic and shared-resource systems. Multiterminal word-processing systems are suited to environments where it may be desirable to share memory files among many operators as well as share peripheral devices among work-stations, thereby maximizing the potential of these devices.

Shared-Logic Word-processing Systems

Quite similar in concept to time-shared computer systems, such systems share the logic, storage, and peripherals of a central computer among a number of keyboard/editing work-stations.

A number of stations may be supported by the processing power of a central minicomputer, and some shared-logic configurations may support up to 30 or more stations. High-speed printers are often employed by such systems. Operator input and editing is usually performed on video display terminals.

Shared-logic systems not only share the logic but also share the cost of the system among the number of stations. Word-processing power that might be cost-prohibitive on a single-station, stand-alone system can be attractive when spread over a number of stations. Thus, shared-logic systems can provide greater computing power and editing capabilities, as well as larger direct memory and storage capacities. Text can be stored, searched, and retrieved as multipage documents and remain in page format and in proper order throughout a number of updates and revisions. A number of word-processing tasks may be performed almost simultaneously on a number of operator stations. For instance, printout may be performed while other text is being input or edited.

Shared-Resource Word-processing Systems

Another type of multiterminal configuration, shared-resource systems encompass a broad range of configurations, but have one thing in common: each work-station within a shared-resource system contains its own intelligence and processing power, dispersed to the operator stations and sometimes the shared peripherals.

The true cost of multiterminal systems must be measured on a per-station basis and on the processing power extended to each station by the system. Prices range from under $25,000 to over $150,000, but the per-station cost is usually in the $10,000 to $20,000 range—similar to the cost of a stand-alone video word processor.

Time-shared Word Processing

This category of text editing often comes under the heading of a service rather than specific hardware. A large central computer, located at a service bureau or in-house, handles many users simultaneously. A typewriter or video terminal located in the user's office is connected through telephone lines or cables to the service's central computer. The terminal electronically communicates with the computers. The service bureau also has high-speed printers for printout of documents, which then can be delivered to the user. For the storage of material, magnetic disks and magnetic tapes are used. Documents requiring immediate access by the hour are often stored on disks, and those that are not are stored on tape.

The principal difference between time-shared services and shared-logic systems is that the time-shared service is an add-on capability to an existing mainframe computer. Shared-logic systems entail a high fixed cost commitment and/or a high initial investment specifically for the text-editing requirement. However, as the text-editing work load increases, the cost for using the time-shared service also increases and could conceivably, in the long run, exceed the cost of the shared-logic system.

In order to provide text editing services to many users simultaneously, the time-sharing service bureaus use large main-frame computers, as opposed to the smaller minicomputers used in shared-logic systems. This enables the time-shared services to provide a more powerful text-editing capability. This capability might include a very sophisticated typesetting program for generating input to a sophisticated phototypesetter, for example.

Personal Computers
Finally, there are the word-processing capabilities of personal computers. A wide variety of software packages are available for most models, although the prices and total functions vary. Word processing is so popular to those who market personal computers that many vendors include the software as part of the standard package.

More important is the fact that such equipment is now affordable to most businesses. Likewise, "user-friendly" machines, which require little to no prior knowledge of either computers or word processing, offer this efficient technology to legions of potential new users. For a relatively modest investment—around $3,000—a personal computer can carry out all or many of the same functions that more expensive dedicated equipment does and with sufficient speed and accuracy.

Major computer and word processor manufacturers now make such equipment and market it through accessible retail outlets, ranging from business computer stores to special departments in large retail stores. To further simplify matters, such retailers also offer in-store or on-site demonstrations and training.

Interfacing Word Processing and Typesetting

It is becoming increasingly feasible to marry word processing and typesetting. Chapter 9 discusses how modern phototypesetting machines are equipped with word-processing capabilities. This means that the typesetter can accept either a typewritten manuscript—possibly generated on word-processing equipment and output on a printer—or a memory disk or other storage medium prepared on a word processor. However, a typesetter accepting word-processing media must be able to interface with a wide variety of noncompatible equipment.

An interface is a method or device for facilitating communication between different machines. The most direct method for interfacing word processing to typesetting is to connect an electronic "reader" for the recorded medium directly to the typesetting machine. The medium is read and the information is translated into data the typesetting machine can understand.

Interfacing can also be accomplished on a service basis. For instance, a service can take IBM MT/ST cartridges and convert them to computer tape and then convert that to IBM magnetic cards.

This interfacing is one of the fastest-growing areas of the publishing industry. The merger conserves paper, is more efficient than typewriting, and reduces printing and postal costs.

Thermography 17

Thermographic printing has been used in the industry since the inception of the process around 1903, and many improvements have been made since then. Basically, its purpose is to produce a three-dimensional relief or "raised" image on paper or other materials, without the use of dies or relief printing plates, but rather with heat-treated ink. This process, however, should not be confused with engraving or embossing (refer to chapter 14), even though the final appearance may be quite similar.

Principles of Thermography

In essence, thermography is strictly an adjunct to the printing process, requiring first that a printed image be made, with ink moist enough to hold the proper amount of heat-fusible powder. All of the wide range of printers' typefaces, layout designs, paper textures, and printing screens may be employed along with it. Indeed, thermography may be combined with all the major printing processes and equipment.

(You may also recognize the term *thermography* from medicine. Completely unrelated to the printing process—other than in the use of heat—it is a technique for detecting and measuring variations in the heat emitted by various regions of the body and transforming them into visible signals that can be recorded photographically. This form of thermography has proved invaluable in diagnosing abnormal or diseased underlying conditions. Incidentally, a similar technique is used to diagnose the insides of engines, and to measure the insulation of buildings.)

In the printing process, thermography is a rather simple technique. Sheets are printed by conventional methods, but the ink must remain tacky and moist on the paper long enough for every line and dot of print-image to be covered with, and hold, the heat-fusible powder. The amount and "tack"of the ink needed will vary with the type of paper and the size of the printed image.

Thermography Equipment

Mechanized thermography employs both manual and automatic equipment. The manual machine is simply a heater, including a conveyor, which carries the printed sheet under the heater. This type of equipment is for short press-runs and experimental work.

Models of automatic machines range in size from those that handle 12-inch-wide sheets to those that handle 30-inch-wide sheets. The 12-inch machines include hand-fed letterpresses and are equipped with six-foot heating sections and long coolers attached to high-speed lithographic presses. The latter is the type typically used in print shops specializing in the production of business cards, social stationery, wedding announcements, letterheads, and envelopes.

During operation, the front conveyor of the automatic thermograph machine is placed on the bed of the press, and the printed sheets are dropped directly onto the conveyor. The sheet then passes under the powdering section, where heat-fusing powder is applied to the sheet; the excess is removed by suction. Next, the sheet passes through the heater unit, and the powder is fused to the ink. Finally, it is carried onto a cooling section and then delivered as a finished printed product.

Thermography Powders

The product's three-dimensional effect may appear glossy, dull, or semidull, and be metallic gold, silver, or copper or else opaque white, depending on the type of powder used. According to the amount of "raise" desired, these powders are available in granulations varying from a very fine #21 to a fairly coarse #30/60. The coarser the powder, the higher the raise, but the less sharply defined the line, too. Usually, a compromise should be established; current usage favors sharp, finely detailed effects to add to the richness of good presswork.

Following is a general guide to proper powder granulation, according to the point-size of the type being used:

Type Size	Powder Granulation
6 to 8 pt	#18
8 to 12 pt	#14
12 to 24 pt	#11
24 to 36 pt	#9
36 pt and beyond	#7

As a rule of thumb, business cards are processed with a #14 powder, letterhead and envelopes with a #11 powder, and larger print areas with a #14 to #11 powder or a combination of the two.

Hard-finished paper stocks can usually be raised with a finer powder than that used on softer vellums or texts. When printing on spongy, absorbent stocks such as newsprint, it is best to run a flat color of ink first and let it dry, and then overprint the thermographic step using either the same color ink or a transparent ink. (For more information on paper and ink, see chapter 11.)

Variations of Thermography

Thermography may be used for printing one-color products or in conjunction with several colors to add emphasis or accent. Small, two-color offset presses have been instrumental in the increased use of thermography to produce two raised colors. For example, if a job calls for a raised metallic or opaque white area and a raised red area, a first run is made with both powders in the thermographic unit; another run is made with a clear, transparent powder. The amount of heat needed to raise the transparent powder is not enough to change the finish of the metallic or opaque white area.

Another method for producing a raised, multiple-color effect is to have all the colors printed and dried first, and then to run the sheets through the thermographic unit, using a transparent powder and transparent ink on the press. Thus, while some of the printed colors are not raised, the raised areas are usually slightly smaller.

As a rule, thermography is used for printing on only one side of a sheet; two-sided thermography is possible but considerably more difficult to accomplish. Special needle inserts are required in the conveyor mesh to keep the first thermographed side out of contact with the heating element. And, in general, a thermographed area should not be on a fold or bleed. If it is, the fused powder is likely to flake or peel.

But when thermographed products such as business cards are folded, folders with rubber rollers are employed, in order to avoid flaking or peeling. Likewise, when stacking the cut cards, there should not be enough pressure applied to flatten the raised printing.

Costs of Thermography

In terms of cost, thermography does not add much to the price of a finished product. Typically, there are no additional labor costs, since a press operator can usually handle both the press and the thermographic equipment. Some printers have installed 180-degree conveyors that return the finished sheets back to the operator.

One pound of thermographic powder will produce approximately 10,000 to 15,000 letterheads and more than 25,000 business cards. For square-inch coverage, a #11 gloss powder will cover nearly 10,000 square inches, while a #14 will cover nearly 14,000 square inches. Therefore, in the end, the cost of thermography is comparable to that of adding an extra color.

The majority of thermographic work is handled by specialized printers. For instance, some print only business cards, others print only wedding invitations, and still others specialize in letterheads and envelopes. Some printers also specialize in applying thermography to metal, plastic, wood, and other materials to create signs and related products. All such specialists generally provide an economical alternative to more expensive embossing, engraving, and other finishing techniques.

Greeting card manufacturers are large users of thermography. They find it adds a certain sales appeal to many card designs without adding much to production costs. The technique may be used to raise captions in flat or metallic colors, to raise color areas applied with a screen base or solid printing, or to raise a complete design, such as a metallic gold on a color stock. As is often the case, the range is limited only by the designer's imagination and the printer's expertise.

Thermography lends itself to industrial applications as well. For example, paper can be made to feel like leather, wood, or brick for use as wallcoverings. Or one might want to print an advertising circular to simulate the look and feel of textured leather or leather shoes. Printers can simulate the texture of an emery board, a grinding wheel, or bricks, as well as wood grains, gauze bandages, cloth upholstery, ceiling tiles, vinyl car-tops, and ceramic tiles. This process can even reproduce oil painting with the feel and appearance of brush strokes. Finally, thermography can be useful as an etching resist in the production of metal nameplates.

New Technology 18 in Printing and Production

If there is one word that summarizes the development of new print production systems, it is *electronics*.

The great technological strides made over the past decade in perfecting and using minicomputers, microprocessors, lasers, fiber optics, and the cathode ray tube, to name a few, have benefited the graphic arts field along with a host of other businesses and industries.

The benefits in printing are twofold: existing techniques have been improved by greater accuracy, higher speeds, simpler operation, and increased capacity; and vast new opportunities and capabilities have been unlocked that were not previously possible by any means.

To be sure, electronics is not the only important benefactor. New emulsion technologies for photomechanical films and printing plates, improved ink pigments, electrostatics for copier imaging, and stronger lightweight papers are all helping to propel the industry into a new age. But it is electronics more than any other single technology that is the key to graphic arts advances. Electronics is revolutionizing typesetting—automating page composition, providing the press operator with timely production data, spanning the continent and the hemisphere with satellite-transmitted copy, and allowing the graphic designer untold freedom of expression in manipulating typography and color artwork.

Exciting advances are being made in every area of the graphic arts. What follows, in a random sampling of such advances, is a discussion of the technology being employed and a description of how it is being applied in print production.

Electronic Pagination

Perhaps because of its very nature and its proximity to art directors, graphic designers, and publishers, electronic pagination is a favorite and very visible example of what electronics technology can do in the graphic arts.

The opportunity to vary entire designs, create instant pages filled with type and graphics, mix and merge editorial copy with display advertisements, and choose from a palette of electronic colors with no more bother than pushing a few buttons captivates nearly everyone's imagination. So pagination, often called full-page makeup, is an ideal barometer of how extensively electronics is changing printing. And while not complete, the change is becoming widespread.

Although there are as many variations and approaches as there are systems, pagination can be defined in terms of the basic operations involved. Copy is entered into a computer memory bank via a conventional keyboard, optical character reader, or video terminal, and held in mass storage, where it can be updated as necessary by calling it back out on an editing terminal. In a totally electronic system, proofreading is done on a video screen, or else a high-speed computer line printer can be used to produce a hard (paper) version of the copy.

At the same time that text copy is being entered, an illustration scanner can analyze black-and-white, continuous-tone photographs and translate them into digital information for mass storage. Within a range, the photographs can be cropped, masked, sized, shaped, electronically altered in density or balance, and screened for conversion to a halftone.

For process color, an electronic separation scanner is used to analyze the original artwork, digitize the information, and hold the data in storage. When requested, the picture information can be electronically altered or improved and made ready for merging with text information.

The actual merging of picture and copy elements takes place at a page-makeup terminal, which, in addition to having a larger video display screen (or a miniaturized representation on a smaller screen), has controls to regulate the entry of text, line art, display type, and halftones, monochromatic or color. By moving a hand-held cursor over a graphic tablet or using a control keyboard, the operator calls from storage the individual page elements and lays them out in whatever format is desired. In certain systems, the exact characters that will appear in the final product are shown on the screen; in others, representation is shown.

As necessary, the operator can retrieve a single line of the article in question, the first few lines, or the entire text. Text can be reset in a different measure, a photograph sized to a different dimension, or a headline point-size changed to fit the space. The computerized system carries out each of these tasks virtually instantaneously, electronically rearranging or "massaging" its storage data at the touch of a button.

It is important to note that the system carries out its functions according to prearranged parameters covering typographic and aesthetic guidelines. In other words, proper hyphenation and justification, widow control, and spacing are automatic, along with additional functions such as formatting, font control, tabular typesetting, and multicolumn layout.

When all page elements are in place and the operator is satisfied with the appearance, the information is transmitted back to storage or sent to a phototypesetter for imaging on photographic paper, ready for the camera and eventual platemaking and printing. Future systems may one day be able to expose a printing plate directly, bypassing the manuscript, galley, and filmmaking stages altogether.

For color work, the steps are fundamentally the same, with two chief exceptions: proofing or previewing, and the exposure of the four necessary separations of film for color printing. The latter step, of course, is performed by the electronic color scanner mentioned earlier; the former, however, assumes several variations. For example, some color users are content to view a color video proof—a cathode-ray tube representation of the color separations that have been made—while others require a color paper or film overlay proof of the result before approving the color or requesting further corrections.

Of course, some very sophisticated systems offer the user capabilities far beyond page makeup, extending even to electronic color correction or enhancement of an overall or very localized area. Integral to such systems is the ability to change colors at the touch of a button or to change designs at the flick of a cursor.

Thus we can see that electronic pagination offers benefits of two types: improvement of existing methods in terms of reduced material use and increased speed, accuracy, and capability; and the unlocking of many new opportunities in color graphics that were not previously possible. Page makeup drastically reduces stripping or image assembly time, eliminates the use of phototypesetting film or paper in galley form, and bypasses the camera step for line work or halftones.

At the same time, artists and designers have at their control the ability to change designs, colors, combinations, and patterns at will, working either from an original scanned into the system or one produced on the screen electronically. Such color graphics represent new vistas in printing, promising the rapid, simple production of exotic, exciting graphics for the needs and wishes of tomorrow's world.

The Laser

The use of lasers in the graphic arts is another captivating subject, probably because of the space-age nature of this unique, monochromatic light source.

The laser's versatility is legendary: it can be linked to electronic controls for digital imaging; be made to expose photosensitive materials, including those that are not silver based; maintain extreme pinpoint concentration for high image resolution; be made to travel over fiber-optic "light pipes" in replacing electrical signals; be used in optical systems that utilize its ability to differentiate at a rapid rate between dark and light reflective images; be pumped up in power to etch or vaporize certain materials; and be turned on and off (modulated) very rapidly.

Lasers can be manufactured in a very wide variety of forms, strengths, and color sensitivities, depending on the source-gas used. High-powered lasers can vaporize metal, while very low-strength ones are designed only to pulse a receiver. All lasers expose diazo and photopolymer materials, some in the ultraviolet wavelength section of the spectrum, some in the visible portion, and still others in the infrared section.

The graphic arts make use of the laser in a number of ways. Laser-based machines can be categorized simply by how each one puts to work the laser light source. One breakdown: scan ("read") only; expose ("write") only; combination scan and expose; and engrave (etch, or physically remove the material).

An optical character reader designed for copy input uses a laser to recognize or read black images on white paper. This is similar to laser units used at a supermarket check-out counter to recognize Universal Product Code symbols on grocery items.

Lasers for exposing sensitized materials can be found in electronic color scanners (only in the output or exposure step, since the monochromatic laser would be useless in analyzing the color original). Exposing-type lasers are also used in certain phototypesetters for imaging sensitized film or paper, in nonimpact xerographic copiers where the laser exposes a selenium-coated drum, and in computer-output microfilm devices.

Some units combine different lasers, one in the input or scan side, the other at the output or expose side. Examples include a photographic facsimile transmitter for sending photos to newspapers, plate-making equipment that scans a paste-up and exposes an offset plate or negativelike material, and an electronic camera that scans an original continuous-tone print and digitizes and screens it for reproduction.

Units that engrave with a laser include one for cutting boards for steel rule dies, another for etching epoxy from gravure cells on an engraved copper cylinder, and one for engraving a rubber roller for flexographic printing.

Reportedly, there are several thousand laser-based units of one kind or another operating in newspapers and magazines throughout the world, in addition to several thousand laser color scanners used by color separators, printing plants, and trade shops. As mentioned earlier, future pagination systems designed to expose a printing plate directly (without the use of intermediate film) will undoubtedly make use of a laser beam. By that time, the laser may well become the most important light source in the graphic arts.

Digital Typesetting

Leading the trend in computer-aided composition is digital typesetting, in which the master characters for the typeface are stored in digital form and called out or generated as needed for typesetting. In fact, some believe that digital typesetting will replace *photo*typesetting in the sense that photographic character masters—grids, disks, drums, or film strips—will be obsolete for all but the most specialized equipment. Imaging is done on a cathode-ray-tube screen, to be projected through a lens onto the photographic film or paper, or directly via a laser onto the film or paper (or perhaps the plate itself, as mentioned earlier). The processes are discussed in greater detail in chapter 9.

The main reason for its rising popularity is that digital typesetting is so fast and versatile. Although manufacture of the digitized type-fonts is costly and the storage requirements quite large, the machinery can modify the output typefaces according to operator command. That is, the characters can be enlarged, reduced, condensed, expanded, slanted forward or backward, or emboldened, all usually from the same font. Equipment models differ, but most offer a broad range of sizes and variations from the same type-font, and most hold on-line an extensive library of different typefaces.

As for speed, a fairly wide selection exists among models, some going as high as several thousand lines per minute. Because of the tremendous production speed and the limited typeface choice available on early models, it was newspapers that initially made use of digital typesetters.

The price of digital typesetting equipment is tumbling rapidly. Already, some units are directly competitive in price, quality, and capability to any high-quality phototypesetters using photographic character masters.

One important note: with the type masters in digital form, and the output characters "painted" digitally by a series of strokes, the machine can be programmed to typeset artwork, logotypes, even halftones, although such graphics reproduction requires extensive data storage. Thus, the digital typesetter is another machine that has the potential and the capability to play a starring role in a future electronic pagination system.

On the other hand, all the attributes of a digital typesetter make it a logical choice among nonprinting companies that are tempted to buy and operate production equipment themselves in order to trim their printing costs or control the process. With this equipment in place, publishers or in-plant printing shops of large corporations may take over yet more steps from the commercial printer or typographic firm.

Satellite Communications

A limited number of newspapers and newsweekly magazines transmit copy and graphics to remotely located printing plants via communications satellites set in geosynchronous orbit 22,300 miles above the earth. Entire magazine pages, with color photographs inserted in position, have been beamed from publishers' offices to printing plants in regional sites.

Satellite systems are, to begin with, ideal for networks of widely dispersed recipients. A receiving antenna can be built and installed for as little as $5,000. Larger, more sophisticated and expensive earth stations are needed in other applications that require high transmission speeds or higher image resolution.

As an example of the use of satellites in the graphic arts, consider the needs of the newspaper industry, which is in a position to benefit from satellite communications in four distinct areas.

First and foremost, the medium will doubtless be used extensively by the newspaper wire services, perhaps even to distribute the news to radio broadcasters. A typical scenario has a nationwide network of small earth stations, one for every newspaper in the country, for receiving news services. Later on, the system could be used for sending national advertisements to individual local papers.

The Federal Communications Commission (FCC) ruled initially to require the licensing of receiving antennae, even though the original legislation was intended to cover the true broadcast capabilities of send–and–receive satellite terminals. The FCC reversed its ruling several years ago, so now no license is required for earth stations using receive-only satellite dishes. This action should have a significant impact on the use, price, and economic feasibility of a network of low-cost, receive-only terminals.

The second area in which newspapers can benefit expands the system to a send–and–receive network rather than a send–only one. In the graphic arts, it includes the sending of full-page copy from a central location to remote printing plants located across states or across the country. Each terminal in such a network would be able to transmit and receive copy or communications signals.

The third potential use of satellite communications is the two–way communications link within a corporation or group of firms. As a result of this send–and–receive network, various receivers would benefit by the sharing of data, which could be called up from data bases in locations throughout the network, to benefit any receiving site that issued a call.

On this corporate communications scene, several large companies have already developed commercial systems to serve the needs here.

Such networks offer document distribution, teleconferencing services, and data communications. All of these uses, which tend to be business services that are generally outside the graphic arts, are subject to continuing FCC rulings regarding coverage. Large newspaper groups and multiple-plant printing corporations obviously are logical users of such systems.

The fourth area in this category can be either a competitive threat or a new business opportunity for graphic arts companies in general and publishers in particular. Referred to as teletext, videotex, or viewdata, such systems may use a satellite, cable television, the telephone network, or fiber-optic cables to transmit information in text and/or color graphics form. Such information includes news, weather, entertainment, electronic banking, teleshopping, and even advertising.

Not surprisingly, the publishing industry—which has the most at stake—is watching developments here very closely. Some publishers have been conducting in-home market tests themselves to see how the public reacts to the equipment (which may consist of a dedicated video screen and keypad or a personal computer), what kinds of information the public wants and is willing to pay for in such systems, and the start-up costs and revenue involved.

Two-way, interactive media have the most potential since they offer more capability than is currently possible with one-way systems, such as conventional television. Satellite communications may someday be interactive, but for the moment the common telephone lines and two-way cable TV lines hold the most promise as tools in an interactive, two-way network for homes and businesses. For this reason, the publishing and broadcasting industries are watching the newly deregulated AT&T since that firm has already made moves to expand its role: It wants to be not only an information carrier but an information provider as well. Today this role is being largely served by publishers and broadcasters, which explains why they are interested in developments involving AT&T and other telecommunications companies.

The situation that exists can logically be expanded to other areas of the graphic arts. Electronic media have the potential to replace ink on paper in some applications. Indeed, several such electronic publications, delivered via desk-top computers, now exist. Just how extensive the eventual replacement or alternatives will be depends on technology, the reaction and preferences of users, and the aggressiveness and resourcefulness of each competing medium.

Ink-Jet Printing

Direct-response merchandising, a modern, improved term for direct mail, is today the prime beneficiary of ink-jet printing because of the ability of the imaging process to vary the information that it prints—an ideal application for individual addressing and personalized messaging on the fly. (Direct mail is the subject of chapter 15.)

Ink-jet printing, with its unique capabilities, can help a lot in those requirements. In this process, a spray of ink droplets is created, charged electrically, and then directed toward the paper or some other substrate. Some of the jet spray is diverted away so that the droplets that do reach the paper form letters and characters.

The most critical aspect to ink-jet printing is that the process is electronically controlled. In other words, the stream of ink droplets is under the control of a computerized data base. Therefore, the image is infinitely variable, changeable, and controllable, at very high speeds. Type sizes and styles may be varied and ink colors changed. The ink-jet unit can be mounted directly on the printing press, to image the recipient's name, address, and personalized message, at often the same rate of speed as the conventional printing press, even on web-fed equipment. Commonly, an ink-jet printing unit can operate at some 600 feet per minute.

Linked with web presses, ink-jet units can produce personalized computer letters in as many as four process colors or more. When automated, on-line finishing equipment is added, the product may be a complete, direct-response package, including sending and return envelopes, coupons, personalized computer letters, and a variety of other items, such as peel-off labels, die-cuts, and scratch-offs.

When ink-jet printing was being perfected, some observers overestimated its impact, calling it the "fifth major printing process" and the "process of the '80s," predicting its replacement of conventional processes. This has not happened. It has found a place in direct-response merchandising. Whether this is merely a toehold for ink-jet printing or its ultimate role in the printing industry remains to be seen.

Computers in Production

Computers have benefited the printing industry for years, but only recently have the electronic descendants of the mainframe computer been miniaturized and made to help out in the production departments as well as the front office and the accounting department.

And what an immediate impact they have had: multiplexed distributed digital systems to monitor make-ready and press operations; microprocessors on a chip that are so small they can be placed almost anywhere; exotic sensors—utilizing microwaves, ultrasonics, and lasers—to detect and analyze vibration, noise, possible problems, and monitor machine performance; and servo controls as standard equipment on new kinds of folders, printing units, reel-tension devices, and roll splicers.

Computers in production continue to proliferate. An automatic film processor was introduced in 1980 that, equipped with a powerful, solid-state microprocessor, can be programmed to process up to five different types of film and to control as many as 11 different functions for each. For example, at the rate of several hundred times per minute, it monitors and adjusts development and drier temperatures, self-corrects its development speed, and varies replenishment times for fix and development as needed. It also has two operating modes designed to save energy, is self-diagnosing, offers help to the operator, and keeps a running total of time, materials used, and chemistry consumed.

A vertical process camera, previously the symbol of mechanical simplicity in the graphic arts, was unveiled in 1981 featuring computerized control and operation. Many of its functions are automatic, including calculations for main, flash, and bump exposures, enlargement or reduction, the proper materials to use, and the correct lens to use for the size change specified.

Some of the newest advances involve putting computers to work on the printing press. Here the data are collected by sensors, which are made to correct an operating problem or compile general or specific running data for use by management. This second use will be covered in the next subsection, on computers in management.

The first use—collection of raw data for use in correcting a problem—is exemplified by the remote-controlled ink fountains found on many modern presses, sheet-fed and web. Here, special densitometers on the press continually monitor the color images; one patented system is a closed-loop design that uses a microprocessor to control the ink keys, instructing them to feed more ink or to reduce the flow. Another system signals the operator when parameters are exceeded, then awaits the operator's instructions on how to proceed.

A computer-assisted bindery control system was devised for use on a magazine gathering line connected to an adhesive binder. It controls gathering-line operation, repairs imperfectly gathered books, and keeps track of and sorts out volumes that cannot be repaired.

Computers in Management

There are two very good reasons why computers increasingly are being put to work in printing management. First, today's manager recognizes that fast, accurate information about company operations is an absolute necessity. Second, new technology has forced down the cost of computer systems so that a manager in a company of almost any size can choose from a variety of ready-made systems or better yet, custom-design one from different components. As the cost has plummeted, the capacity and capabilities have skyrocketed.

Computers are proving to be useful tools in four general business areas in printing, apart from their obvious and documented applications on production machines.

Accounting and Bookkeeping

Stated in simple terms, the intent here is to assign labor and material charges to the right accounts via the particular jobs being performed and then to pay the employees for their work. Reports or statements involved include jobs in production, labor and materials assigned by cost center, invoices, accounts receivable, purchasing and accounts payable, payroll, balance sheet, income statement, cash-flow reporting, cash disbursements, and daily deposits, among others. The main benefit here is accurate, timely reporting, compared with hand or semiautomated methods.

Estimating

In many ways, this step is the key in the overall production operation of a printing plant, because it requires that job planning be completed first. In other words, an estimator, using basic information about the job provided by the customer, must determine the best combination of labor and materials to produce the job. Then, using price lists and rate schedules, he or she assigns costs and calculates how much the job will be sold for. Computerizing this step may involve anything from storing price lists or costs for labor or materials to automating all possible routes of jobs through a plant based on job criteria. The benefits include streamlining of job loading, optimum production path, inclusion of all job charges, and accurate, timely reporting of job parameters.

Production Control
A manager monitors the performance of production departments to determine strengths and weaknesses, problems, productivity, and inefficiency. Much of the information is available by adding a few lines of programming, so that he or she can chart averages and trends of either individuals, cost centers, or entire departments. Or data can be collected concerning individual jobs. Further, the manager can connect inventory control of raw materials and finished goods, or decide to expand this to purchasing, all to apparent benefit.

Management Information
In the broadest sense, the previous three areas all contain the kind of information a manager needs to run a business effectively. In addition, there are other data that can help sharpen a manager's skills involving internal production rates and the customer's needs and wants. Computers can be made to compile reports on customers, sales, markets, products, production departments, production costs, profits and losses, volume by salesman, most- and least-profitable jobs or customers, and actual costs versus estimated costs.

Steady progress has been made in all areas mentioned, but unquestionably the greatest growth has been in production data collection via a network of sensors mounted on the equipment. Some data collection is automatic, some is input manually by the machine operator. Whichever the method, it is but the first step in putting computers to work in printing production and management.

From this brief discussion, it can be seen that print production is today in a state of flux as the industry tries to apply new technology to its problems and to reach out for new opportunities.

The novelty of exotic new devices and materials has vanished in the graphic arts, replaced by a dedication to make them work—to improve existing techniques and to make possible untold wonders in the years ahead.

Index